Hans Magnus Enzensberger was born in Nuremberg in 1929. He is a professor, journalist, editor, critic and prize-winning poet. He has lived in Munich since 1979.

HANS MAGNUS ENZENSBERGER

Civil Wars

From L.A. to Bosnia

The New Press, New York

The New Press

Published in the United States by The New Press, New York
Distributed by W. W. Norton & Company, Inc.,
500 Fifth Avenue, New York, NY 10110

ISBN 1-56584-208-1
LC 94–67608

Established in 1990 as a major alternative to the large,
commercial publishing houses, The New Press is the first full-
scale nonprofit American book publisher outside the university
presses. The Press is operated editorially in the public interest,
rather than for private gain; it is committed to publishing in
innovative ways works of educational, cultural, and community
value that, despite their intellectual merits, might not normally
be considered "commercially" viable. The New Press's editorial
offices are located at the City University of New York.

Printed in the United States of America
94   95   96   97   9   8   7   6   5   4   3   2   1

CIVIL WAR

I

GHASTLY EXCEPTION, GHASTLY RULE

ANIMALS FIGHT, but they don't wage war. Only man—unique among the primates—practises the large-scale, deliberate and enthusiastic destruction of his fellow creatures. War is one of his most significant inventions, so the ability to make peace is something to aim for in the future. The most ancient of our traditions, the heroic myths and legends, deal almost exclusively with killing and death. It is not just on technological grounds that war is waged at the closest possible range. Psychologically, it is much more satisfying to vent your hatred on the enemy you know: that is, on your immediate neighbour. Civil war is not merely an old custom, but the primary form of all collective conflict. Its classic account, the *History of the Peloponnesian Wars*, was written 2,500 years ago and has never been bettered.

'Cultivated' war waged between nations and against external enemies is, on the other hand, a relatively recent development. It calls for the existence of a professional warrior caste, the establishment of standing armies and the distinction between military and civilian, and leads to the development of complicated rituals, from the declaration of war to surrender. The nineteenth century saw some rationalization of the slaughter: on the one hand, advances in weapons technology and general conscription led to an increased death-toll; on the other, states attempted to subject their wars to regulation by civil law. These rules were first expressed in the Hague Land Warfare Convention of 1907. Seen in this light, civil war seems to be the exception to the rule, an irregular form of warfare. The Prussian general von Clausewitz devoted not a word to it in his classic work, *On War*. To this day, there is no useful Theory of Civil War.

It's not just that the mad reality eludes formal legal definition. Even the strategies of the military high commands fail in the face of the new world order which trades under the name of civil war. The unprecedented comes into sudden and explosive contact with the atavistic. Old anthropological questions come to the fore. Which is stranger: killing people you know, or destroying an opponent you have absolutely no conception of, not even a false one? For the bomber crews of the Second World War the enemy was a pure abstraction; even today the teams in the underground bunkers on permanent alert for the order to launch the missiles are hermetically isolated from any inkling of the havoc that pressing the button will wreak. This is so perverse that it makes even the most absurd civil war seem almost normal by comparison. It is generally the rule, rather than the exception, that man destroys what he most hates, and that is usually the rival on his own territory. There is an unexplained linkage between hating one's neighbour and hating a stranger. The original target of our hatred was probably always our neighbour;

only with the formation of larger communities was the stranger on the other side of the border declared an enemy.

II

Old Scores, New Mob

THE END of the Cold War has called time on our notion of the West as an idyll protected by force. The balanced deadlock of Pax Atomica no longer exists. Until 1989 two nuclear-armed superpowers eyeballed each other implacably, with the divided Germany at the seam of their confrontation. The terrors this precarious situation evoked are already half forgotten. Others have appeared to take their place. The most obvious sign of the end of the bipolar world order are the thirty or forty civil wars being waged openly around the globe. We cannot even be sure of their exact number, since chaos is uncountable. But the signs are that things will get worse before they get better.

No one was prepared for this turn of events. No one knows what to do. It could be that we have entered an entirely new phase of politics. To grasp its significance, we need to look back at the civil wars of the past. The most damaging and the most wearisome in the history of Germany, and one from which the country has probably never quite recovered, was the Thirty Years War. Two-thirds of the population are said to have lost their lives.

That war was fuelled and manipulated by external powers, in common with most of the larger civil wars in recent history: the war of the American South against the North, the Whites against the Reds in Russia, the Spanish Falange against the Republicans. In all these instances there were regular armies and fronts; the central command structures attempted to carry out their strategic objectives in a planned way through strict control of their troops. As a rule there was political as well as military leadership, following clearly defined goals, and ready and able to negotiate when necessary.

But while the classic war-between-states tends towards the monopolizing of power, and by every measure strengthens the apparatus of the state, civil war is characterized by the constant threat that discipline will break down and the militias dissipate into armed bands operating on their own account.

Individual warlords declare their independence; military headquarters lose control of the warring groups as the government loses political control. But in the wars in the US, in Mexico, in Russia and in China, both sides were always in a position to negotiate, to claim victory or to surrender. In each case the conflict ended with the consolidation of a new regime in the conquered territory and the establishment of the rule of law. It is doubtful whether today's civil wars will have a similar outcome.

In the age of imperialism there was no internal conflict that did not immediately take on an international dimension. So-called *Realpolitik* ensured that every civil war was fuelled and exploited by external forces. The parties to the conflict acted as puppets in a larger game. For the world powers it was about extending their spheres of influence and their colonial empires. One only has to think of the repeated attempts by Europeans and Americans to get a foothold in China, of the interventions in the wake of the Bolsheviks' October Revolution, or of the Spanish Civil War, which has been described, not without some truth, as a dress rehearsal for the Second World War.

Throughout the seventies the superpowers held fast to this logic. They waged a series of surrogate wars the length of Africa, Asia and Latin America, and meddled in every internal conflict that held out any promise of advantage in their zero-sum game. They did their utmost to escalate these conflicts, to within a hair's breadth of starting a third world war.

It was only with the end of the Cold War and the disintegration of the Soviet Union that this particular variety of foreign policy gave up the ghost. Word got around, not just in Moscow and Peking but in Washington too, that brotherly aid costs rather more than it brings in return. The economic winners of recent times were those countries which hadn't taken part in the game. Today the old *Realpolitik* lies broken among the ruins of an imperialistic cast of mind that belongs to the nineteenth century. It will gain no ground in the new world market.

War, once the simplest means of enrichment, has become bad business. Capitalism has realized that state-regulated slaughter does not pay sufficient dividends. Of course the new-found enthusiasm for the politics of peace now shown by governments of the industrialized countries owes more to this sober insight than to any sudden moral conversion. We are not used to regarding capital as a force for peace, and no doubt many of its factions still look forward to booming rates of growth from the business of war. And yet the export of weapons accounts for only 0.006 per cent of world trade—in effect it has become of secondary importance and can, when necessary, endure the imposition of sanctions. Countries torn by civil war pay no dividends in the long run. They are punished by the withdrawal of investment. This late realization finds its political expression in the peace missions of the United Nations.

Today's civil wars ignite spontaneously from inside. They need no external powers to fan their flames. Until recently they came disguised as revolutionary uprisings or wars of national liberation. Only since the end of the Cold War have we been able to see them for what they really are.

Take the civil war in Afghanistan. For as long as the country was occupied by Soviet troops, the situation invited interpretation along Cold War lines. Moscow was supporting its surrogates, the West the Mujahedin. On the surface it was all about national liberation, resistance to the foreigners, the oppressors, the unbelievers. But no sooner had the occupiers been driven off than the real civil war broke out. Nothing remained of the ideological shell. Foreign adventurism, the integrity of the nation, true belief—all that was revealed as a mere pretext. The war of everyone against everyone else took its course.

Similar developments can be seen everywhere, in Africa, in India, in south-east Asia, in Latin America. Nothing remains of the guerrilla's heroic halo. Once ideologically armed to the teeth and exploited by their shadowy backers, today's guerrillas and anti-guerrillas have become self-employed. What remains is the armed mob. All the self-proclaimed armies of liberation, people's movements and fronts degenerate into marauding bands, indistinguishable from their opponents. The crazed alphabet they hide behind, FNLA or FLNS, MPLA or FMLA, cannot disguise the fact that no goal, no plan, no idea binds them together other than the strategy (which hardly merits the name) of plunder, death and destruction.

III

MOLECULAR CIVIL WAR AND THE ABSENCE OF CONVICTION

WE LOOK at a map of the world. We pinpoint wars in distant lands, preferably in the Third World. We talk of underdevelopment, differences in cultural maturity, fundamentalism. We tell ourselves that this unintelligible struggle is happening far away. But we are deluding ourselves when we reason that we are at peace simply because we can still collect our bread from the baker's without being blown away by sniper fire. The reality is that civil war has long since moved into the metropolis. Its mutations are part of everyday life in our cities, not just in Lima and in Johannesburg, in Bombay and in Rio, but in Paris and Berlin, in Detroit and Birmingham, in Milan and Hamburg. The combatants are no longer just terrorists and secret police, Mafiosi and skinheads, drug dealers and death squads, neo-Nazis and cowboy security guards. Even ordinary members of the public are transformed overnight into hooligans, arsonists, rioters and serial killers. And as in the African wars, the combatants are becoming younger by the day.

Civil war isn't something we've imported from

abroad. It's not some virus we have allowed to infect us. It comes from within, and it always starts with a minority: it is probably enough if one person in every hundred wants to make civilized co-existence impossible. In the industrialized countries the overwhelming majority still prefer peace. Civil wars have not yet infected the mass of the population; they are still molecular. But, as events in Los Angeles show, they can escalate at any time to epidemic proportions.

But can we really compare the one with the other? The Chetnik with the second-hand furniture dealer from Texas who climbs a tower and begins firing into the crowd with a machine-gun? The Liberian warlord with the skinhead who smashes his beer bottle over the head of an innocent pensioner? The rioters in Berlin with the jungle fighters in Cambodia? The Chechen mafia with the Sendero Luminoso? And all of this with the normality of small-town life in Germany, Sweden or France? Is all this talk of civil war an empty generalization, or plain hysteria?

I fear that, in spite of the differences, there are common denominators: the autistic nature of the perpetrators, and their inability to distinguish between destruction and self-destruction. In today's civil wars there is no longer any need to legitimize your actions. Violence has freed itself from ideology.

Compared with the present lot, earlier combatants were true believers. They set the greatest store by killing, or being killed, in the name of some ideal. No matter how repulsive their world view (as it used to be known), they held to it 'with iron resolve', 'fanatically', 'unshakeably'. The disciples of Hitler and Stalin followed the gospel of their leaders with shining eyes, and when it came to the crunch, no crime was too big.

Even the guerrillas and terrorists of the sixties and seventies thought it expedient to justify their actions. With fly-posters and proclamations, in pedantic catechisms and bureaucratically formulated confessions they explained the ideological reasoning behind their deeds. Today's lot seem to find all that unnecessary. The complete absence of conviction is striking.

The combatants in Latin America's civil wars don't think twice about slaughtering the farmers they claim to liberate. They are unembarrassed by, and feel no need to justify, their alliances with drug barons and the secret service. The Irish terrorist uses pensioners as living bombs and blows up cars full of children. The preferred victims of today's civil wars are women and children. The Chetniks aren't the only ones who boast of massacring all the patients in one hospital; it seems that everywhere the aim is to dispose of the defenceless. If you don't have a machine-gun you count as vermin.

The protagonists are almost exclusively young men. Their behaviour demonstrates the extent to which the patriarchal system has been eroded. One of its most ancient traditions was the grouping together of young males into bands whose function was to harness their testosterone-fuelled energies, their impulsive actions and their blood-lust through rites of initiation. They were subjected to tests of courage and had to demonstrate their fighting skills. In all this a strict code of honour was enforced. Its most basic rule was that the challenger, be he Samurai or Wild West hero, criminal or rebel, had to match himself against the strongest and most dangerous opponent, and at the very least an equal. Such notions are foreign to today's hooligans. A new manliness has come to the fore. It may seem to glory in cowardice; but that would be an exaggeration, for it is unable to distinguish between bravery and cowardice. And that is symptomatic of autism and the loss of conviction.

Such characteristic defects are all the more visible in wars waged in the name of ethnic conflict. Scraps of justification are paraded, like rags from the wardrobe of history, with the operatic staging so beloved of those in power. Second- and third-hand propaganda is trotted out—like that produced by the Serbian Academy, for example—in an attempt to simulate conviction. But these mobs have no real need of a pretext.

We should note that the wars of the nineteenth century which led to the formation of today's nation-states were more than simply irrational brawls. By focusing only on the emotive chauvinism that characterized old-style European nationalism it is easy to overlook the constructive contribution it made. After all, it helped bring about the drafting of constitutions, the abolition of serfdom, the emancipation of the Jews, the establishment of the rule of law and the enfranchisement of the general population. Achievements of this kind are far from the minds of today's warrior gangs. Modern-day nationalists are interested only in the destructive forces that ethnic differences can unleash. When they talk about the right to self-determination, they mean their right to determine who will be allowed to survive on their territory, and who will not. Their principal concern is the extermination of the worthless. Nothing could be less important to warriors in Angola, in Somalia, in Cambodia than the fate of their alleged blood-relatives; they seem content to ruin their livelihoods, to blow them up and put them to the sword.

The ideological basis for Islamic fundamentalism is also, one suspects, a good deal less concrete than the West believes. Any intelligent Muslim will tell you that it has nothing to do with high religion. It is much more about a radical present-day reaction to the build-up of pressures towards modernization. The caricature of Saddam Hussein posing as a pious Muslim is wholly blasphemous. The same can be said of most of the regimes in the Maghreb and the Middle East. In their wildest ambitions they betray their fixation with their sworn enemy, the West. Its deadliest inventions—atom bombs, missiles and poison-gas factories—are the very focus of their envy. In the meantime the various sects, factions and militias are at each others' throats. What we see is not conviction, but its facsimile.

The molecular civil wars in our cities are similarly lacking in reason. Gang warfare in the North American ghettos has nothing to do with the historical class struggle. Not even the theory of black versus white provides a satisfactory rationale, for victims of muggings, robberies and murders are blacks more often than not. It wasn't the homes of the rich that were the target of the riots in Los Angeles; the perpetrators set fire to buildings in their own community, including the oldest surviving bookshop in America, owned by blacks, and the office of the most militant local politician in the neighbourhood. In gang wars everywhere, it is a case of the have-nots shooting at each other.

And so to Germany's own representatives in the molecular civil war. We call them radical right-wingers or neo-Nazis, and we think we know what to expect of them. But even here the ideological label is no more than a charade. The juvenile murderer who attacks the defenceless, when asked to explain his motives, responds with the following: 'I didn't really think about it.' 'I was bored.' 'There's something about foreigners I don't like.' And that's it. He knows nothing about national socialism. He's not interested in history. The Swastika and Hitler salutes are optional extras. His style of dress, his taste in music and his immersion in video culture are American through and through. He wears his Nazi T-shirt with jeans. The thug calls himself a 'skinhead' and is proud of this English name. *'Deutschtum'* ('Germanness') is a slogan devoid of content which serves only to fill the empty spaces of his brain.

In the place of Turks and Vietnamese, his targets could just as easily be disabled people, the homeless, the mentally ill, children or the elderly. Or even, if he weren't too much of a coward, West or East Germans, depending on where he lives. He wouldn't find it hard to choose between *Deutschtum* and his motorcycle, between *Vaterland* and the disco. Indifferent to his own future, it is no wonder that he doesn't care a jot for his country.

The same goes for right-wing radicalism in its political guise. The triumphant song-and-dance over the bankruptcy of communism disguises the fact that the right-wing agenda came to grief some time ago. No sooner does the radical right get anywhere near a position of political power than it becomes clear it has nothing to offer. What passes for its programme is an illusion that is economically unworkable. Most industrial countries are integrated to a large extent in the world market and completely dependent on it. National autarchy, racial or ethnic homogeneity and independent political efforts would soon lead to famine. Right-wing internationalism is an absurd concept. That is why what is called the New Right is incapable of a coherent European policy. 'Germany for the Germans' is more than just a provocative slogan: anyone who took it seriously would have to dispossess all foreign-owned companies and close Frankfurt airport. It is obvious that the spokesmen of the Right don't believe in their own bluff. Their old world view has disappeared without trace, and left only an empty longing for aggression in its place.

IV

SELFLESSNESS AND SELF-DESTRUCTION

MOLECULAR AND regional civil wars have more than just
the combatants' autism in common. Their participants
must also be selfless. In 1951, Hannah Arendt wrote:

> I suspect there has never been a shortage of hate
> in the world; but . . . [by now] it had grown to
> become a deciding political factor in all public
> affairs . . . This hate could not be targeted at any
> one person or thing. No one could be made
> responsible—neither the government, nor the
> bourgeoisie, nor the foreign powers of the time.
> And so it seeped into the pores of everyday life
> and spread out in all directions, taking on the
> most fantastical, unimaginable forms . . . Here it
> was everyone against everyone else, and above
> all against his neighbour . . .
>
> What distinguishes the masses today from
> the mob is their selflessness, their complete dis-
> interest in their own well-being . . . Selflessness
> not as a positive attribute, but as a lack: the feel-
> ing that you yourself are not affected by events,

that you can be replaced at any time, anywhere, by someone else . . . This phenomenon of a radical loss of self, this cynical or bored indifference with which the masses approached their own destruction, was completely unexpected . . . People were beginning to lose their normal common sense and their powers of discrimination, and at the same time were suffering from a no less radical failure of the most elementary survival instinct.

Arendt was writing of the period between the two world wars, describing the situation which led to the establishment of the totalitarian regimes. The relevance of her analysis to today's situation is plain. But in contrast to the thirties, today's protagonists have no need for rituals, marches and uniforms, nor for agendas and oaths of loyalty. They can survive without a Führer. Hatred on its own is enough. If in those days terror was the monopoly of totalitarian regimes, today it has reappeared in de-nationalized form. The Gestapo and the OGPU are superfluous when their infantile clones can do their work for them.

Every carriage on the underground can become a miniature Bosnia. You don't need Jews to have a pogrom; counter-revolutionaries aren't the only elements that need cleansing. It's enough to know that someone supports a different football club; that his greengrocer's shop is doing better than the one next door; that he dresses differently; that he speaks a different language; that he wears a headscarf or needs a wheelchair. Not to conform is to risk death.

Their aggression is not directed only at others, but at

themselves. It is as if it were all the same to them not only whether they live or die, but whether they had ever been born, or had never seen the light of day. However huge the genetic pool of stupidity might be, it is not big enough to explain this urge to violent self-destructiveness. And the nexus of cause and effect is so obvious that any child could understand it.

Howls of protest at the loss of jobs are accompanied by pogroms which make it obvious to any thinking capitalist that it would be senseless to invest in a place where people go in fear of their lives. The most idiotic Serbian president knows as well as the most idiotic Rambo that his civil war will turn his country into an economic wasteland. The only conclusion one can draw is that this collective self-mutilation is not simply a side-effect of the conflict, a risk the protagonists are prepared to run, it is what they are actually aiming to achieve.

The fighters know very well that there will be no victory. They know that, eventually, they will lose. And yet they do everything in their power to up the stakes. Their aim is to debase everybody—not only their opponents, but also themselves.

A French social worker reports from a housing estate in the suburbs of Paris:

> They have destroyed everything: letter-boxes, doors, stairways. The health centre, where their younger brothers and sisters receive free medical treatment, has been demolished and looted. They recognize no rules of any sort. They smash doctors' and dentists' surgeries to pieces and tear down their schools. When they are given a new football pitch, they saw down the goalposts.

This picture of molecular civil war resembles the full-scale event down to the last detail. A reporter tells how he witnessed an armed band smashing up a hospital in Mogadishu. This was no military operation. No one was threatening the men, and no shots had been heard in the city. The hospital was already badly damaged, equipped only with the bare essentials. The perpetrators went about their business with a fierce thoroughness. Beds were slit open, bottles containing blood serum and medicine were shattered. Then the men, in torn and dirty camouflage uniform, set about destroying the few remaining pieces of apparatus. They did not leave until they had made sure that the single X-ray machine, the sterilizer and the oxygen generator were no longer usable. Each one of these zombies knew that there was no end to the war in sight. They all realized that within hours their lives might depend on whether there was a doctor around to patch them up. And still their obvious intent was to eliminate even the smallest chance of survival. One is tempted to call this the *reductio ad insanitatem*. In the collective running amok, the concept of 'future' disappears. Only the present matters. Consequences do not exist. The instinct for self-preservation, with the restraining influence it brings to bear, is knocked out of action.

One is reminded of Freud, who after much speculation felt he had no alternative but to postulate the existence of a death drive, whose primary goal was the destruction of the individual's own life, with the destruction of the lives of others as a secondary aim. His hypothesis could never be tested empirically and has remained vague. But even the concept of the survival instinct is problematic, even naïve. It might govern the behaviour of bacteria and plants, but it fails in the higher animals, and there isn't a lot in history to support it. After all, millions have died as saints and martyrs, heroes and fanatics, ignoring the dictates of self-preservation. Pessimistic thinkers like de Maistre have always recognized the central significance of sacrifice, and made a virtue of repression. It is possible that all religions have their origins in personal sacrifice; ever since the gods were banished from the world, men have never been short of some higher purpose in whose name they would kill and die. We might even wonder whether 'culture' is dependent on this ability to put causes before ourselves.

There are still people around who, in the old-fashioned sense of the word, act selflessly: aid workers who take personal risks; opponents of regimes, such as Jan Palach, or the nameless Buddhist monks of Indo-China, who burned themselves alive for their convictions; but also cult leaders and fanatical priests who believe they will be rewarded in heaven for the extinction of their own lives.

In war, however, the reins are held not by these few, but by those who have lost everything they might have had to sacrifice. What gives today's civil wars a new and terrifying slant is the fact that they are waged without stakes on either side, that they are wars *about nothing at all.* This gives them the characteristics of a political retrovirus. We have always regarded politics as a struggle between opposing interests, not only for power, for resources and for better opportunities, but also in pursuit of wishes, plans and ideas. And although this power-play invariably results in bloodshed and is often unpredictable, at least the intentions of those involved are usually obvious. But where no value is attributed to life—either to one's own life or to the lives of one's opponents—this becomes impossible, and all political thought, from Aristotle and Machiavelli to Marx and Weber, is turned upside down. All that remains is the Hobbesian ur-myth of the war of everyone against everyone else.

V

LABYRINTHS OF MEANING, BLIND ALLEYS

FACED WITH the inexplicable, the temptation to find the simplest possible explanation becomes irresistible. It is no surprise that, of all the available interpretations, politicians and leader-writers reach for the weakest they can lay their hands on. In this they are simply following established party lines. Anyone reviewing their efforts might as well refer to the abridged version.

Conservative commentators never tire of evoking an imaginary golden age when common decency and discipline were supposedly the order of the day. They lay the blame for the breakdown of order in the world firmly on the emancipation movements of the past 200 years and on the decline of traditional authority. They offer salvation in a return to virtues which had their roots in class-ridden patriarchal societies. How and by what means such longings might be realized in the latter phase of industrial civilization is never quite explained.

The Left has fared no better. In the twilight of social democracy, Rousseau has triumphed once again. It is therapy, rather than the means of production, that has been nationalized. Social work is the last refuge of the curious notion that man is basically good. Here the best pastoral intentions enter into strange alliances with old-fashioned theories of environment and socialization and a slimmed-down version of psychoanalysis. Its proponents, in their boundless good nature, excuse the aberrants from all responsibility for their actions. It's never the fault of the offender, always his environment: his home, the consumer society, the media. It's as if every murderer were handed a multiple-choice questionnaire which he had to fill out as best he can:

Mum didn't want me;
My teachers were far too authoritarian/liberal;
Dad came home drunk/never came home at all;
The bank gave me too much credit/closed my account;
I was spoiled/neglected as a child/at school/at work;
My parents got divorced too soon/too late;
In my neighbourhood there weren't enough/there were too many leisure activities;
So there was nothing else for me to do but arson/robbery/mugging/murder.
(Please delete whichever does not apply)

At a stroke we can rid the world of crime, since there are now no criminals, only clients. Even Hess and Mengele, were they to appear today, would be regarded as victims in need of sympathy and, perhaps, psychotherapy paid for by the state. Following this logic, only the therapists can handle the moral questions, because only they possess the necessary understanding. Everyone else becomes a mere recipient of welfare.

Compared to the political kitsch of this common-place, even the crudest materialistic crisis theories seem plausible. At least they are based on economic fact and can thus be tested. Only an idiot would argue that just because Marxist analysis is out of fashion, it is no longer useful. Few dispute that the world market, now that it is no longer a vision of the future but a global reality, produces fewer winners and more losers as each year passes. This is not confined to the Second and Third Worlds, but applies equally in the core capitalist countries. Where, there, whole countries, or even whole continents, drop out of the international exchange system, here, increasing sections of the population can no longer keep up in the competition for advantage that gets more brutal by the day.

If you imagine a map of the world that shows the geographical distribution of the 'superfluous' masses—on the one side regions of underdevelopment in their varying degrees and, on the other, zones of underemployment in the metropolitan centres—and compare these with the sites of the many civil wars, you will notice a correlation. The general level of violence, you might conclude, is no more than the desperate reaction to a hopeless economic situation.

And yet the political consequences the Marxist theoreticians predicted have not come about. So far, their theories have been proved wrong. International class war has not broken out. Those on either side of the famous 'fundamental contradiction' are less likely than ever to want to seek global confrontation. The losers, far from regrouping under a common banner, are hard at work on their own self-destruction, and capital is retreating from the battlefields wherever possible.

In this context we must attempt to dispel the stubborn notion that exploitation is merely a question of unfair distribution, as if we were talking about the equal or unequal sharing-out of a cake. For this equation is flawed. It appears most often in the form of the assertion that 'we'—the industrialized West—live at the expense of the Third World; the reason we are so rich is because we exploit them. Those who beat their breast in this manner don't have much time for the facts. Just one statistic will do: Africa's share of world exports is around 1.3 per cent, Latin America's around 4.3 per cent. Economists who have looked into this doubt whether the inhabitants of the richer countries would even notice if the poorer continents simply disappeared off the face of the earth. Nothing, not the debt crisis nor the fluctuating price of raw materials, the flight of capital nor protectionism, can alter this catastrophic imbalance.

Theories that ascribe the poverty of the poorest exclusively to external factors offer cheap sustenance to our sense of moral indignation. They also have a further advantage: they unburden the rulers of the poorest countries from their responsibility for the misery, and place it solely on the shoulders of the West (which has recently been renamed the North). Africans who have seen through this trick have said that there is only one thing worse than being exploited by the multinationals, and that is not being exploited by them. They no longer see their chief political enemies in the centres of capitalism, but in the political gangster-class that has been systematically ruining their countries for decades. No rational person believes that the big banks have been running the twenty-year civil war in Chad, or that Idi Amin was a pawn of the CIA, or that the Tamil Tigers are mere puppets of the Pentagon. In spite of this, the notion persists in Europe that there are no protagonists, only string-pullers. Thus neither Serbs nor Croats are responsible for the war in the former Yugoslavia; instead it is the fault of some minister of state in Bonn who supposedly wanted to recreate the Greater German Empire.

Insane attributions of this sort play an important part in molecular civil war, only here it is usually foreigners—Jews, Koreans, Latinos or gypsies—who fall victim to the paranoia of those who regard them as the authors of their misery. Such conspiracy theories only obscure the appalling truth: in New York as well as in Zaire, in the industrial cities as well as in the poorest countries, more and more people are being permanently excluded from the economic system because it no longer pays to exploit them.

If this is so, it casts doubt on the theories which see all the world's conflicts as crises brought about when one culture encounters another at a different stage of its development. These would have us believe that global modernization is an unstoppable linear process; that civil wars are like any other undesired by-product of the contradictions that progress brings with it. Underdevelopment, fundamentalism, tribal feuding are put down to backwardness. The most common version of this view finds its highest expression in the claim that other societies 'live in the dark ages'. And thus, invented forms of tradition, like some ethnic costume ball, are taken at face value without any closer examination.

This view of development obviously contains the seeds of hope for those who subscribe to it. If only the traditional mentality and means of production can be overcome, they say, then nothing will stand in the way of a happier future. The backward societies need only follow the path of their more advanced neighbours in order to catch up with them. Unfortunately a model based on this philosophy of history is itself old-fashioned. For the drive towards modernization comes to grief when those who have been 'left behind', wherever they find themselves, realize they are in a hopeless situation. On ecological, demographic and economic grounds the modernization gradient never levels out; on the contrary, the difference in degree between the most and least developed widens year by year.

'In his innermost self, the victim of colonization recognizes no authority. He is humiliated, but not convinced of his humiliation.' Using the example of European colonial rule, Franz Fanon showed thirty years ago that *The Damned of the Earth* rebel not only against need and hunger, but against the continuing humiliation they are exposed to. The thought is not a new one. It originates in German philosophy. Hegel's famous fable put it this way: the original condition of human society is war, not only over available resources, but also for peer-group recognition. This war is fought to the bitter end, until the loser either dies or surrenders. In this case he becomes the servant of the winner. But dialectic insists that it is the servant, rather than the master, who will change the world. He achieves this through his labour, to the point where the master becomes dependent upon him. Once this stage is reached, he forces his own recognition. Historically this came about with the French Revolution. Only then could the universal, homogeneous, constitutional state come into existence, where every citizen was guaranteed the recognition of his fellows. With this, freedom and emancipation was achieved for all; the story comes to an end with Napoleon, and the realization of equality.

You don't have to be a Hegelian to see that the longing for recognition is a fundamental anthropological fact. But the notion that it has ever been realized is illusory. It is something that the overwhelming majority of those alive today can only dream about. The attraction of terrorist regimes in the twentieth century is probably connected to the fact that all have promised the humiliated the opportunity to force others to recognize them— as a community, as a classless society, as a church— through the power of violence. And each time they keep their promise by denying this same recognition to everyone else.

After the fall, the struggle begins again, only now, in the terminology of Franz Fanon, the humiliated no longer have their colonial masters: 'The conquered are persecuted men who constantly dream of becoming persecutors themselves. The old resentments, buried deep in the collective memory, come to life again in tribal feuding. The conquered throw themselves into acts of revenge . . . The literal self-destruction of a collective is therefore one of the ways in which the conquered vent the physical strain of colonization.'

Hegel takes the expression 'recognition' literally and attempts to establish it objectively. The man who feels humiliated will never let matters rest there. It is one thing to postulate equality—the rule of law has, in some countries, succeeded in abolishing the crassest forms of repression. But the desire for recognition, first in the cities and then across the whole world, has gathered a momentum that a certain philosopher in 1806 could never have dreamed of.

Every community, even the richest and most peaceful, continually creates new inequalities, slights, injustices, unreasonable demands and frustrations of all kinds. The more freedom and equality people gain, the more they expect. If these expectations are not fulfilled, then almost anyone can feel humiliated. The longing for recognition is never satisfied. Newspaper editors know the story well enough: the ghetto kid who wants a pair of designer training shoes enough to kill for them; the office worker who fails in his ambition to become a pop star and robs a bank or shoots into a crowd of people to get his own back for the humiliation he has suffered.

A last attempt at an explanation, the most depressing of all, concerns the unprecedented growth in world population. As early as the fifties, Hannah Arendt made the connection between the ease with which totalitarian regimes were able to implement their murderous schemes and the population explosion with its ensuing homelessness and landlessness of people who were, in the sense of a utilitarian categorization, 'superfluous'. It is as if the value they place on the lives of others depreciates as the birth rate increases.

Such an attitude is difficult to understand. But we don't need statistics—of population, of migration, of numbers of refugees—to realize just how crowded the planet has become. We can see it every day. Joblessness, homelessness, inner-city decay, refugee camps, all prove that there are simply *too many* of us. And we react psychotically by striking out blindly in all directions.

The tendency is at work everywhere. Even apparently ordinary people take it upon themselves to do away with the 'superfluous' masses, a group to which they themselves belong. The steps they are prepared to take differ only in degree, and depend on the means at their disposal. While the arsonist has only his bottle of petrol, the dictator can offer poison gas and rockets. The instigators of civil war aim beyond so-called ethnic cleansing; their ultimate intention is complete depopulation. If they can't achieve total annihilation, they will settle for driving their enemies out of the country, using them as a demographic weapon against the outside world. As punishment for its defence of the remains of a civilization, a third party is charged with the care of the victims. The gang leaders regard the population as tiresome waste to be disposed of by someone else.

It is difficult to know where in this train of thought the search for meaning stops and contempt for human life begins. The threshold is crossed once we reason that humanity is unselfconsciously following a biological imperative, designed, as it were, to reduce the population of the planet to a level it can support.

There is no lack of voices propounding this view; scientists argue it and self-proclaimed representatives of the natural order applaud their arguments, often choosing to support their case with reference to the legendary experiment in which more and more rats were forced to inhabit an ever smaller space. According to this logic, civil wars and other forms of self-mutilation are nothing more than mechanisms which ensure the survival of the species.

These ideas only characterize the hubris and megalomania of their sponsors. For years the work of certain biologists has lent support to totalitarian regimes. The aims of eugenics and the achievements of the medical experimenters will not easily be forgotten. We saw the consequences in the concentration camps. The comparison with rats is no accident. But quite apart from the moral vulnerability of the biological argument, it is also intellectually defective.

To propound it is to claim to see humanity from the outside, a perspective which is nonsensical on epistemological grounds. It is simply not valid for a human to attempt to speak from the standpoint of a virus or a galaxy.

Biology adds nothing to our understanding of civil war.

VI

EVIDENCE AND SELF-EXPERIMENTATION

THE BEGINNING is bloodless, the evidence circumstantial. Molecular civil war starts unnoticed; there is no general mobilization. The amount of rubbish on the side of the streets increases gradually. Piles of syringes and broken bottles appear in the park. Monotonous graffiti is daubed on the walls, its only message one of autism. Classroom furniture is smashed up, front gardens stink of shit and urine—tiny, muted declarations of war which any experienced city-dweller can interpret. Soon the signs become clearer. Tyres are slashed, emergency telephones have their cables cut, cars are set on fire. In one spontaneous incident after another, rage is vented on anything undamaged, hate turns on anything that works, and forms an insoluble amalgam with self-hate.

Youth is the vanguard of civil war. The reasons for this lie not only in the normal pent-up physical and emotional energies of adolescence, but in the incomprehensible legacy young people inherit: the irreconcilable problem of wealth that brings no joy. But everything they get up to has its origins, albeit in latent form, in their parents, a destructive mania that dares not express itself except in socially tolerated forms—an obsession with cars, with work and with gluttony, alcoholism, greed, litigiousness, racism and violence in the home.

It is difficult to say which party in this cauldron of aggression is most dangerous. One's perception changes. A man who doesn't drive a car tells his story: 'This is what happens when I catch the late evening train home. The carriage is almost empty and badly lit. An old man is sleeping in a corner; two fellows who have had a few drinks are talking at the other end of the compartment. The pair next to me have probably just finished their overtime. The train stops and four guys in their twenties get in, wearing the usual leather jackets and boots. They're making quite a lot of noise and talking in a language I don't understand, Arabic perhaps. Their behaviour seems provocative, and, as they move through the carriage, they appear to be looking for someone to pick on. They come closer and I immediately feel threatened. They stare at me. I sense I'm going to be attacked. Then they move on and my gaze falls on the other passengers. Their faces are embittered, seething, distorted with a peculiarly ugly rage. The phrases they spit out I recognize only too well. Even the old man has woken up and murmurs something about hanging them up and shooting them down. And now it's not the foreigners I'm afraid of, but my own people.'

'My daughter's school trip has had to be cancelled,' says another, 'because there are three Turkish girls in her class; the other parents won't let their children go because they think it would be taking too big a risk. This proves that certain public spaces are simply off limits; you can't go there without endangering yourself. This is not new. Years ago the Kreuzberg district of Berlin was ruled by 200 people who called themselves *autonoms*, which in this context meant: human society does not exist for us. Their aim was to silence the rest of the population, and they were at the time generally successful in this. They created an area in which there were no rights, and where censorship, fear and blackmail ruled. The institutions retreated; what was left of the civilian population was gradually driven out.

'There are similar areas in Eastern Europe and in what used to be East Germany. Isn't it ironic that what was once the Zone has in this way become a Zone again? Might rules in many parts of the cities. The police feel outnumbered and are scared to go in, so becoming silent accomplices. There is talk of "liberated" areas, as the perpetrators succeed in liberating themselves from civilization and its burdens.

'These circumstances lead to a double migration: on one side, the immigration of gangs of thugs in neo-Nazi costume and, on the other, the flight of those they threaten, in the first instance foreigners and ideological opponents, but, in the end, anyone who refuses to submit to the state. The outlook for the future is the complete disintegration of territory. As we have seen in the United States, de-industrialization is a significant factor in this process. Normal living conditions dissolve, to be replaced either by protected residential areas with their own security guards, or by slums and ghettos. The mandate of authority, police patrols and the court of law does not hold in the parts of the cities surrendered to the mobs. They become uncontrollable.

'The border zones also play by their own turbulent rules. Smuggling, trafficking and criminality have radically altered the standards of these neighbourhoods. The illegal immigrants don't help matters; in most cases they are accustomed to different social norms and can summon up little enthusiasm for the traditional way of doing things. But even among the locals standards of civilized behaviour fall off sharply. They are replaced by the elementary rules of force. Just as Saddam Hussein revoked the rights of the Iraqi people, here all internal commitments, written and unwritten, are being extinguished. In the end only a gun counts for anything.'

Those who are threatened have only two options: flight or self-defence. A privileged minority finds its own form of escape; it can retreat to a hideaway in the sun, take cover in a second, or retirement, home, start a commune in the country, or join some remote sect. For the penniless millions, escape takes the miserable form of forced emigration and asylum-seeking.

Those who don't flee wall themselves in. Everywhere in the world international frontiers are being fortified to keep the barbarians out. But even in the inner cities archipelagos of safety are being constructed, and these will be defended to the last. There have long been bunkers for the fortunate in the great cities of America, Africa and Asia, guarded by high walls topped with barbed wire. Sometimes whole city districts can only be entered with a special pass. Barriers, electronic cameras and trained dogs control access, machine-gun installations on watch-towers secure the surroundings. The parallel with the concentration camp is obvious, only here it is the outside world that is regarded by the inmates as a potential extermination zone. The privileged few pay a high price for the luxury of total isolation: they have become prisoners of their own safety.

More and more people are beginning to arm

themselves in the vicious circle that is part of the dynamic of civil war. Where the state can no longer enforce its monopoly on violence then everyone must defend himself. Even Hobbes, who concedes almost unlimited executive authority to the state, says of this situation that: 'The subjects' duty towards their sovereign lasts only as long as he is able to protect them through his power. Man's natural right to protect himself when no one else is in a position to do so cannot be withheld by any treaty.' The reasons behind the retreat of the state vary enormously. In the beginning it is often out of cowardice or some tactical calculation, as in the Weimar Republic and latterly in the reunited Germany. At a more advanced stage of the molecular civil war it might be because the police and judiciary are no longer masters of the situation; the overfilled prisons have become training camps for the combatants. In other cases it is because the state has lost all legitimacy, as in the former Soviet Union. One step further—viz the former Yugoslavia—and it is the regime itself that is organizing the armed bands.

Those who can will waste no time in hiring mercenaries to take the place of the police. A sign of this is the growth of the so-called security industry. The bodyguard has become a status symbol. Security firms are even hired by state-owned concerns to protect the infrastructure. Wherever the local citizenry are unable to pay for hired guards they form neighbourhood watch or vigilante groups. Where this isn't possible, people will sooner or later buy themselves handguns; this is already evident in the United States, where an individual's right to carry arms has become a national ideology.

Civil wars, from the molecular to the full scale, are

infectious. As the number of people untouched by war steadily falls, because they have died or fled or attached themselves to one side or the other, the participants become more and more difficult to tell apart. They begin to resemble each other both in their behaviour and in their moral attitudes. In the war zones of the cities, the police and the army act like any other armed gang. Anti-terrorist units operate preventative shoot-to-kill policies, and drug addicts and small-time criminals find themselves facing death squads who are the mirror image of their supposed opponents. The lumpenproletariat gives rise to a corresponding lumpenbourgeoisie, which in its choice of means copies its enemy. It is the same with the epidemic of wars. Aggression and defence become indistinguishable. The mechanism resembles that of the blood feud. More and more people are pulled into the whirlpool of fear and hate until the situation becomes quintessentially antisocial.

'We don't know what has happened to us.' That is the most common phrase we hear from the survivors of Sarajevo. When all other explanations fail, self-experimentation presents one of the few remaining possibilities of getting to the bottom of the matter. Bill Buford, an American writer, thought he would try it out. In his book *Among the Thugs* he tells how he became part of the mob. This is a report from the latency phase of the civil war. It is set in a football stadium:

'While I couldn't say that I had developed a rapport with any one of "them" yet, I did find that I was developing a taste for the game . . . It was, I see now on reflection, not unlike alcohol or tobacco: disgusting, at first; pleasurable, with effort; addictive, over time. And perhaps, in the end, a little self-destroying.'

In the following scene, the accommodation with violence reaches its climax:

> There were now six of them, and they all started kicking the boy on the ground. The boy covered his face. I was surprised that I could tell, from the sound, when someone's shoe missed, or when it struck the fingers and not the forehead or the nose. I was transfixed. I suppose, thinking about this incident now, I was close enough to have stopped the kicking . . . But I didn't. I don't think the thought occurred to me. It was as if time had dramatically slowed down, and each second had a distinct beginning and end, like a sequence of images on a roll of film, and I was mesmerized by each image I saw . . .
>
> With that first exchange, some kind of threshold had been crossed, some notional boundary: on one side of that boundary had been a sense of limits, an ordinary understanding—even among this lot—of what you didn't do; we were now someplace where there would be few limits, where the sense that there were things you didn't do had ceased to exist . . . It was an excitement that verged on being something greater, an emotion more transcendent— joy at the very least, but more like ecstasy. There was an immense energy about it; it was impossible not to feel some of the thrill. Somebody near me said that he was happy, very happy, that he could not ever remember being so happy.

VII

ASSUMPTIONS OF INNOCENCE,
MORAL MINEFIELDS

JUST THE mention of civil war sooner or later turns into a kind of self-experimentation. No bones are broken; and yet every disagreement about the civil war fuels the war itself. I am not neutral. I have been infected. I feel the rage, the fear and the hate building up inside me. I am deeply involved in my subject. My brain is flooded with chemical messengers I know nothing about. I am in danger of losing control of the thoughts that come into my head.

It is impossible to have a linear discussion on this theme. Merely stating your own position fans the flames of conflict. There is no Archimedean point. I have stepped into an intellectual and moral minefield. I have to move with great care. But I know that although I might, if I'm lucky, find my way through, I'll never be able to clear the field. I don't see eye to eye with anybody, not even with myself. Because I happen to have been born in Germany, I still remember, fifty years on, crouching in a cellar, wrapped in a blanket. To this day, I can distinguish the bark of flak from the scream of an aerial bomb. Sometimes I am haunted by dreams in which I hear the rising and falling tone of sirens. I well remember the half-queasy, half-apathetic terrors of the air raids. And the grown-ups who cowered on the benches in the cellar, at whom these 'terror-raids' were aimed; they were the 'innocent civilians'. Every time I hear these words I fall into broody silence.

As the civil war reaches its climax, it becomes clear that the majority of the population never wanted it to happen. They remain silent. No one pays any attention to them. Wherever they see the slightest opportunity they turn from the fighting and run. Most of the women seem to spend all their time either grubbing around in the ruins for a handful of flour, for firewood, for a few potatoes, or dragging away their children. Old people poke at the ashes of their burned-out huts, tired men bury the dead. These images, and worse, are familiar to everyone. These people aren't gunmen or torturers. Their faces are not scarred by hate for their neighbours. They are grey with exhaustion.

But it wasn't always like this. A strange transformation had occurred in the 'innocent civilians' who sat in the cellars while all around them phosphor bombs turned the city into a sea of fire. I remember how their eyes lit up every time the Führer spoke and let them know what he had in mind: 'a titanic and unprecedented struggle,' a fight to the bitter end. I remember too how a few years earlier these same people had stood by and watched while the synagogues burned to the ground. Without their enthusiastic support the Nazis could never have come to power.

Anyone who thinks that this applies only to the Germans is an idiot. Neither the molecular civil war on our own doorstep nor the inferno beyond our national borders can ignite without the 'piercing energy', the 'joy', the 'ecstasy' Bill Buford speaks of. It always starts with hysterical jubilation, whether it is on the football terraces or on the streets of Rostock or Brixton, Baghdad or Belgrade. Often the warmongers emerge from the polls with triumphant majorities and occasionally their positions are confirmed in subsequent elections.

Later, much later, in a pattern that seems all too familiar, responsibility for the crime is palmed off on some clapped-out ringleader of the past. But who was it who fed and nourished the perpetrators, who applauded them and prayed for them, if not the 'innocent civilians'? The sniper in camouflage; the concentration camp guard; the killer droning Nazi slogans, folk-songs or a quick prayer: all are representatives of their society who feed on its rage, its cruelty, its lust for revenge. Only when they feel the deadly consequences of their actions, and when their omissions begin to touch their own lives, does the hour of the innocent strike.

VIII

CULTURE OF HATE, MEDIA TRANCE

HAPPY THE man who can talk himself into believing that culture can safeguard society against violence. Even . before the start of the twentieth century the artists, the poets and the theoreticians of the Modernist movement showed that the opposite was true. Their predilection for crime, for the satanic outsider, for the destruction of civilization is notorious. From Paris to St Petersburg the intelligentsia of the *fin de siècle* dabbled with terrorism. The early Expressionists longed for war as much as the Futurists. Even after the First World War the glorification of violence increased rather than diminished. Large parts of high culture extolled the return to barbarism. The writings of Sade were elevated to the status of a cult which continues to this day. Ernst Jünger promoted the cleansing power of the steely blade, Céline flirted with the anti-Semitic mob and André Breton declared that the purest surreal act consisted of 'going into the street armed with a revolver and shooting blindly into the crowd for as long as possible.' Just how seriously one ought to take the European avant-garde's cult of violence is a matter for debate. Its provocative acts derived as much from a sense of self-loathing as from a deep hatred of the status quo. Its members were probably also compensating for their own sense of powerlessness in the face of a headlong rush towards modernization which they must have felt threatened their right to recognition. Besides which we must take into account their tendency towards posturing which as performers they were no strangers to. Perhaps we ought to regard them as an early-warning sign: in their obsession we get a glimpse of what is to come. In any case they weren't influential enough to agitate for civil war.

The communist and fascist ideologues were not nearly as ineffective as, enraptured, they set about the millionfold extermination of bourgeoisie, peasants, Jews, gypsies and every other conceivable variety of deviant. A large part of the Yugoslav intelligentsia has shown that the production of hatred and the preparation for civil war is still one of the principal concerns of the creative artist.

The industrialization of popular culture has led to a situation in the richest countries where the cult of violence and *nostalgie de la boue* have become common property in every sense. The expression 'avant-garde' has acquired an ominous connotation which its spokesmen can hardly have thought possible. They surely can't have imagined that hoards of deadbeat artists would take their élitist fantasies seriously and even put them into practice.

Meanwhile the massacre has become entertainment for the masses. Films and videos compete to turn the professional killer, the hostage-taker, the serial murderer into the darling of the public; the grant-aided civic theatre trundles along helplessly in the wake of the horror movie with its own blood-and-guts productions. The mirror-image claims to be a 'no-holds-barred confrontation' which 'spares the viewer nothing', it is 'fearlessly provocative' and 'healthily shocking'—a piece of critical hypocrisy which is seen through immediately by the public. In the middle of all this lurks dear old rock music, eternally young, with groups who call themselves Public Enemy or Slayer, Demolition or Endsieg, Brutal or Guns N' Roses, which sold fifteen million copies of its debut album, *Appetite for Destruction*.

Vandalism is traded high even in the art market. The tautological squiggles of the graffiti scribblers roll uninterrupted into the galleries. The desire to shock is often on show in the art world. Naturally, we are dealing here with vicarious pleasures whose attraction owes everything to maintaining a safe distance from reality. It would be naïve to suggest a link of cause and effect when it is obvious that the artist who acts tough is simply attempting to curry favour.

Even though they occasionally dress up in the emblems of some run-down aesthetic, the perpetrators have long since ceased to rely on their heroes of old. The media trance in which they find themselves is not a matter of imitation, but the direct feedback between image and reality. There are countless criminals who feel that they are not really involved in their actions. They convince themselves that they didn't actually beat other people to death, that it was all 'television'. Theories of simulation are borne out in the most absurd way by some people's inability to distinguish between reality and film.

To a certain extent the media magnify the person who has become unreal and give him a kind of proof of existence. This is a consequence of the pathological self-lessness that Hannah Arendt diagnosed. Every halfwit with a petrol-filled beer bottle in one hand and his other arm raised in a Hitler salute can hope to make the front page of the *New York Times*, and watch his previous night's work on the evening news: burning houses, mutilated corpses, late-night sittings and crisis committees. This is how television works: as a single, huge piece of graffiti, an artificial replacement for the autistically-shrunken ego.

IX

LUCKY DIP, GUILTY CONSCIENCE

NEVER HAS there been so much talk of human rights as now; nor has the number who know of them only as a phrase ever been so large. The Universal Declaration of Human Rights, passed unanimously by the General Assembly of the United Nations in 1948, presents in its preamble and thirty articles a long catalogue of political and social rights, including the right to life, liberty and personal security, the right to freedom of thought and of religion, the right to freedom of expression, the right to social security and to work, and the right to a standard of living which guarantees health and well-being. As if that weren't enough, it also says: 'Every person is entitled to a social and international order in which the above rights and freedoms can be fully realized.'

At the time, the communist countries, South Africa and Saudi Arabia abstained from the vote, which I suppose was at least truthful. All other countries signed the text without hesitation, including those where persecution and censorship, repression and torture were the order of the day. Even today, you have to reckon on an absolute majority of dictatorships in the General

Assembly; the democracies represent a tiny minority, and many of them have waged colonial wars in the years since 1948 or supported terrorist regimes whenever it served their needs to do so.

Four-fifths of the world's population live in conditions that make a mockery of the declaration's rhetoric; every year another hundred million join them. The outlook for them is even more bleak than it was for their parents. Against this background, the proud formulations of the UN seem a little cynical. The subjects of the Soviet state felt mocked in the same way by Stalin's constitution of 1936 which promised basic rights to everyone.

The Europeans and North Americans have only themselves to blame if the world takes them at their word on the subject of human rights. It is they, after all, who have made it a political talisman, first with the American Declaration of Independence of 1776, and then in the *Déclaration des droits de l'homme et du citoyen,* signed in Paris in 1789. Not long afterwards, in 1793, during the Terror, they went as far as declaring *le bonheur commun,* general happiness, a goal of the state. Of course sympathy for one's fellows, a readiness to help them and a longing for universal justice are no rarer in those parts of the world that have not produced declarations on all that is good and worthy than they are in Europe and North America. The poor countries of Africa have given asylum to more civil war refugees than the European Community; there are democratic movements in all continents; and the rich countries, from Japan to the United States, are without equal when it comes to xenophobia and racism.

But the rhetoric of universalism is a specific trait of

Western societies. They expect their decrees to apply to everyone, indiscriminately and without exception. Their universalism recognizes no difference between near and far; it is absolute and abstract. The obligation it places on all of us is, in principle, unlimited. Here the declaration reveals its theological origins which have survived all attempts at secularization. We should all be responsible for everyone else; this implies that we can all become more like God; it presupposes omnipresence, or even omnipotence. But since our scope for action is finite, the gap between the claim and the reality opens ever wider. Soon you cross over into objective hypocrisy and, in the end, the universalism reveals itself as a moral trap.

The once silent accusation has become eloquent. It goes like this: everywhere in the world people are being massacred, dying of hunger, being driven from their homes, tortured, raped, and you just stand by and do nothing, you go about your daily business wringing your hands. It is directed at governments but also at the man on the street, at the great powers as well as the little people. And there is no doubt that we have all become spectators. That is what differentiates us from earlier generations who, if they were not themselves victims, attackers or eyewitnesses, would have had to rely on rumours, on legends. You could only know by hearsay what was happening elsewhere. As late as the middle of this century, the general public knew little or nothing of the greatest crimes of the epoch. Mass murder was a state secret. There were no television cameras in the extermination camps.

Today, in contrast, the murderers are happy to give interviews and the media are proud to be where the killing is. Civil war has become a TV soap. The combatants lay their crimes before a public audience. They obviously expect to gain prestige from their actions. In this, they emulate the metropolitan hijackers, gangsters and hostage-takers whose demands so often include the right to star in front of the TV cameras; and the media ensure that they are granted this wish. The duty of reporters is no longer merely to inform; they make it brutally clear who's who and what's what, while the commentator supplies the necessary tone of outrage.

The accusation carries another unavoidable, subliminal message that widespread fear has become commonplace, and that the unthinkable can and does happen, at any time, anywhere. So why not here? Every policeman is familiar with the phenomenon of copycat crime, and it has now become a political fact of life. In this sense the media, intentionally or not, act as propagandists for the crimes they report.

If these images of terror don't make terrorists out of us, they turn us at least into voyeurs, and subject each one of us to an enduring moral blackmail. Once we have become eyewitnesses, we are open to accusations: now that we know the situation, what are we going to do about it? Television, the most corrupt of all media, is transformed into a paragon of morality.

The fact that we are now expected to do something (but what?), to intervene (but how?) has all manner of consequences. It is 'we' who go around speaking up for human rights; 'we' who invented the guilt trip; 'we' who count as rich and have always thought of ourselves as civilized. Morality is the last refuge of Eurocentrism.

Anyone who has ever tried to discuss the problems of Northern Ireland, or of the Basque country, with a Kurd or a Tamil knows that he is likely to come up against a blank wall of indifference. The response he ought to expect runs: 'What do I care about your stories?' The man from Asia will tell you that he has other problems to deal with. We should think twice before condemning this answer. Even the citizens of Ohio, Piedmont or Hesse must feel hopelessly overloaded in the face of the unintelligible shoot-outs on their television screens. But the sheer weight of information with which we are bombarded makes any kind of intelligent analysis impossible. No one but a specialist with nothing else to do can be expected to remember the names of the 150 nationalities liberated by the fall of the Soviet Union.

And yet the evening news presumes that every supermarket checkout girl can distinguish between the Ingusch and the Chechens, the Georgians and the Abkhasians. We are expected to remember the names of gangsters before we can pronounce them, and to concern ourselves with Islamic sects, African militias and Cambodian factions whose motives are and will remain a complete mystery to us. Anyone who isn't up to this counts as a hard-hearted ignoramus and a selfish member of the affluent society who couldn't care how others are suffering.

As the recipients of this message, we feel uncomfortable. Some of us are plagued by feelings of guilt, but unless we become professional aid workers, our scope for action is severely limited. Many of us give to charity. We, in turn, are accused of trying to buy ourselves a moral alibi. Good deeds are simply a palliative, an attempt to dodge the burden, a cheap way to a clear conscience— the high priests of virtue never reveal exactly what one ought to do.

The theory that our sensitivity to a given stimulus can be heightened by gradually increasing our exposure to it is at best naïve. On the contrary, the likely effect will be psychological and cognitive overload rendering the spectator immune to every stirring of conscience. He feels incompetent and powerless; he curls up into a ball and switches off. The message is repelled or simply denied. This form of internal self-defence is not only understandable, it is unavoidable; who can prescribe the 'correct' response to the daily slaughter?

Beyond this denial lies what a pharmacologist would call the 'paradoxical response' which happens when a substance is used incorrectly or in the wrong dose and has the opposite effect on the patient to that intended. When the moral demands made on an individual are consistently out of proportion to his scope for action, he will eventually go on strike and deny all responsibility. Here lie the seeds of brutalization, which may escalate to raging aggression.

X

CRIES FOR HELP, VOICES UNHEARD

THE SITUATION overwhelms not just the individuals involved but existing political systems as well. There is still no international mechanism for stemming the growth of civil wars—neither foreign policy nor the world authorities, to say nothing of the European Community, are yet up to the task, although they are condemned from every quarter for not intervening everywhere. Today, UN soldiers are stationed in more than fifteen countries. The political costs are astronomical, the mandates contradictory, the successes dubious. In so far as the origins of the conflicts are at all rationally comprehensible, they cannot be sorted out by peace missions, because any attempt at mediation assumes that the participants are willing to make peace. Usually, both sides are determined to carry on fighting to the point of mutual self-destruction. The peace envoy who wants to spike their guns can count on being torn apart by mobs from both camps. Aid organizations are routinely threatened, supply convoys are ambushed and their contents plundered. Mediators are treated with suspicion and blackmailed, aid workers are taken hostage, negotiations sabotaged; peace-keeping troops are shot at with live ammunition. The governments that dispatch them don't even allow them to fire back in self-defence, let alone consider a military solution.

Sanctions and embargoes are threatened, but never enforced. A completely watertight blockade, backed by force of arms, has never been tried, although it might be extremely effective. Any civil war isolated from all contact with the outside world, deprived of its supplies of energy and ammunition, its lines of communication cut, without money, transport and food, would fizzle out within months. But it is precisely the effectiveness of this recipe that prevents its use. Before the first timid steps have been taken the intervening coalition finds itself in the dock, accused, in its efforts to isolate the warring bands, of unavoidably targeting the 'innocent civilian population'.

As a consequence, the authority and credibility of all the parties involved diminishes by the day, as the clamour grows for more to be done. Why are we intervening in country X when country Y is being left to its own devices? The factions on the losing side do not understand why the outside world doesn't rush to their aid. When it doesn't, hope is transformed into disappointment, expectation into indignation, even into rage and thoughts of revenge. There are precedents for this in the early part of the century, as in this extract from the diary of a writer in Petrograd in 1919:

> If they murder us, if they raze Russia to the ground, these ignorant, unappreciative Europeans . . . The senseless, criminal practice of entente will continue . . . All of us who live in

Russia would love to see England experience at first hand what it is doing to us . . . In all the history of the world, there has never been anything like it. All analogies are useless. A great city is killing itself. And all this under the eyes of Europe which will not lift a finger to save us: it is so steeped in blood that it has become either idiotic or satanic . . . This is the exact formulation: if, in twentieth-century Europe, a country with such a phenomenal and previously unparalleled general system of slavery can exist, and Europe accepts it or fails to understand it, then Europe itself must be doomed, and it will deserve its fate.

The allocation of blame spreads like the wars themselves. If you refuse to intervene militarily, you are accused of discrimination and barbarism. And with this, the anti-colonial argument loses more ground. On the one hand, it preaches sovereignty, independence and non-intervention; on the other, the might of the West is allocated a universal responsibility, so that the party that is really to blame appears both as prospective saviour and invader. This has already led to some voices calling for recolonization in the form of a mandate.

This extreme offers the protagonists an easy cover. For in civil wars nothing is ever the fault of the local leaders and their supporters among the masses; the blame always lies with others, preferably from abroad. It doesn't seem to bother anyone that this denies great chunks of the world's population the right to speak for themselves, as if they were mere puppets, incapable of independent action. This fits well with the feelings of superiority of the once colonial rulers, who always treated those they ruled as children: it wouldn't do to let them get their hands on anything dangerous; they need someone to speak up for them. The only possible supervisory power is the West, which is then responsible for all the consequences, regardless of what is done or not done.

In the confusion of this intervention and that intervention there is the risk that one important distinction relating to the rights of peoples will be overlooked: the difference between wars of invasion and internal conflict. The most recent example of this distinction was seen during the Gulf war. Iraq first invaded a weaker neighbour, then attacked Israel, a distant state and one totally uninvolved in the conflict, with missiles.

The coalition against Hitler would never have come together had he been satisfied with killing his own fellow citizens. Nor was Stalin opposed as long as he was terrorizing only the Soviet people. It was when he attempted to export his horror that the Cold War began.

The universalist ethic cannot come to terms with this elementary distinction. It demands unlimited deployment, everywhere and at any time. But this does not add up. There comes a point when the governments of the intervening powers reach the limits of what they feel is politically acceptable to their own electorate. The war in the former Yugoslavia has shown that the Europeans are neither willing nor able to impose a peaceful settlement. Even the United States, the last world power, is finding the role of universal policeman too heavy a burden. All the guilt, all the money, all the soldiers on the planet, will not suffice to put an end to all the world's civil wars.

PRIORITIES, CONTRADICTIONS

IN 1931, a brilliant research scientist by the name of Kurt Gödel proved that no mathematical system can be entirely without internal contradictions. In this, he succeeded, once and for all, in turning on its head the deeply held conviction that mathematics alone can deliver us from the quagmire of inconsistency. Since this is quite beyond even the most refined logicians, how then can we expect to solve the ever-increasing ethical contradictions by a simple axiomatic system?

It's time to bid farewell to these fantasies of omnipotence. In the long run no one—no country and no individual—can avoid coming to terms with the limits of his own responsibility, and setting priorities. (Perhaps we ought to explain what a priority is. Some people pretend to be more stupid than they really are as soon as they encounter an argument that doesn't fit their view of the world. So: the word priority means more than a simple either–or, more than just the choice between mutually exclusive alternatives. Where to begin? Where can I engage my efforts most effectively? Which of these options should take precedence? So much for semantics.

Clear enough? Here ends the digression.)

This is a difficult and unpleasant decision to have to take. It runs counter to our ideological traditions and presents us with bitter choices. To suggest that our scope for action should be both finite and relative is to risk being pilloried as an isolationist. But deep inside, we all know that our foremost concerns must be for our children, our neighbours, our immediate surroundings. Even Christianity spoke of loving our neighbours, not people miles away.

The search for the limits of our own responsibility can produce thoroughly positive by-products. There are existing models for it in adoption and godparenthood. They prove that it is not merely physical proximity, never mind blood relationship, which counts, but rather the forging of a close bond between the helper and the helped. This enables, beyond the concentration of physical and emotional energies, the establishment of a concrete relationship in the place of an abstraction. Every attempt to help and to allow oneself to be helped brings with it inevitable conflicts; it can only be borne when the parties know each other.

But the setting of priorities has a darker side, and it would be dishonest to ignore it. The word 'triage' is of French origin and means selection or choice according to quality. The expression first occurs in the nineteenth century, in field medicine. After the great battles, doctors, faced with the difficulties and dangers of transporting the patients, had to choose how to treat the wounded. The limited capacity of the field hospitals and the shortcomings in the available surgical facilities meant that a system of triage, based on a division of the wounded into three categories, became more or less the rule.

Those whose injuries were slight were given only first aid, and had to make their own way back behind the lines. Soldiers whose wounds looked hopeless were left to their fate. Effective medical treatment was given only to those whose need was acute and who had reasonable prospects of recovery. The doctors' dilemma is obvious. They had to live with the moral risk that every life-and-death decision carries with it. Similar situations are commonplace today in intensive care and transplant medicine. Only a mischief-maker could equate triage with the fascist system of selection, for here the choice is about saving lives, not destroying them. Universal solutions which would allow us to treat all patients equally are not in sight. It is foreseeable that this kind of predicament will become more common and even more thorny in the future.

Such extremes make clear the agonizing hopelessness involved in every ethic of responsibility today. Whether it is famine aid, political and military intervention, forced expulsions or mass migrations driven by the urge to escape from misery, the fact is that all imaginable options end in the logic of triage, whether we admit it or not. Even the gradualist approach, the setting of priorities, the limiting of responsibilities, however plausible their justification, do not guarantee a way out of the minefield. At best they count as a stopgap. Against the promise held out by universalism, they can offer only their workability and lack of self-deception.

No one would dispute that universal solidarity is a noble goal. Those who are determined to achieve it are to be admired. But a look at our own country shows us how uneasily the desire to stand up for justice everywhere sits with the barbarity of the everyday. We

Germans cannot parade ourselves as guarantors of freedom and champions of human rights while mobs of German thugs and arsonists are spreading fear and terror day and night.

We cannot solve the situation in Kashmir; we know little of the struggle between the Sunnis and the Shiites, between the Tamils and the Sinhalese; whatever is to become of Angola must, in the first instance, be decided by the Angolans. And before we put a spoke in the wheels of the warring Bosnians, we ought to mop up the civil war in our own country. Our priority is not Somalia, but Hoyerswerda and Rostock, Mölln and Solingen. That is something we *are* capable of doing, a position we can expect everyone to support. That is what we have to answer for. But you don't have to be German to understand what that means: *Hic rhodus, hic salta!* First things first. Everywhere we look the war is on our own doorstep.

XII

LITTLE MIRACLES

NOT EVERYONE is running amok. Not everyone wants everyone else extinct. Once the combatants have achieved their aims and the whole country lies in ruins and the dead have been buried, the real heroes of the civil war step forth. They are late to arrive. Their entrance is unheroic. They don't stand out. They won't be on television.

In an improvised workshop, artificial limbs are being made for amputees. A woman is looking for rags to use as nappies. Shoes are fashioned from the tyres of a bombed-out car. The first water-pipe is patched together, the first generator starts up. Smugglers get hold of some fuel. A postman appears from nowhere. A mother who lost her children hangs a hand-painted sign outside her hut and opens the first café in the neighbourhood. A bishop gathers together a ragged band of mercenaries, and sets up a car repair workshop in the shed beside the church. Civilian life begins. It is unstoppable, until the next war.

Even the small-scale, molecular civil war doesn't last for ever. After the street battle, the glazier arrives; the telephone in the vandalized kiosk is reconnected by two men with pliers and connection blocks. Emergency doctors work through the night in overflowing clinics to save the survivors.

The persistence of these people is close to miraculous. They know they cannot put the world to rights. Only a corner of it—a roof, a wound. They even know that the murderers will be back, in a week or in a decade. Civil war doesn't last for ever, but it constantly threatens to start again.

They wanted to make Sisyphus an existential hero, an outsider and a rebel of tragic proportions, larger-than-life and crowned in diabolical glory. Perhaps that is wrong. Perhaps he was something much more important, an everyday figure. The Greeks interpreted his name as the grammatical superlative of *sophos*, clever; Homer even called him the cleverest of men. He wasn't a philosopher, he was a trickster. The story goes that he caught Death and bound him hand and foot. And Death remained defeated until Ares, the god of war, freed him and handed Sisyphus over to him. But Sisyphus overcame Death a second time and managed to return to earth. They say he reached a ripe old age.

Later, as a punishment for his human understanding, he was condemned to push a heavy boulder up the side of a hill for the rest of time. The name of this stone is peace.

EUROPE IN RUINS

A few days before I left Luanda, I was taken by American friends to dine in a black-market restaurant. We ate at outside tables in a little enclosure on the street. The clientele all looked more or less as if they were black-market profiteers themselves. We were sitting right next to the rail that fenced us in from the street, and I had my back to this, so that, absorbed in conversation, I did not notice at first that a crowd had gathered behind us and people were reaching in to grab things from our plates. But the management soon sent out a bouncer, who knocked down an old woman with a blow on the head, and drove back the mob, mostly women and children, some of whom disappeared, while others, keeping their distance, stood dumbly and stared at the diners.

Here in Beirut, refugees are lying on all the steps, and one has the impression that they would not look up even were a miracle to take place in the middle of the square, so certain are they that none will happen. One could tell them that some country beyond the Lebanon was prepared to accept them and they would gather up their boxes, without really believing. Their life is unreal, a waiting without expectation, and they no longer cling to it: rather, life clings to them, ghostlike, an unseen beast which grows hungry and drags them through the ruined railway stations, day and night, in sunshine and in rain; it breathes in the sleeping children as they lie on the rubble, their hands between bony arms, curled up like embryos in the womb, as if longing to return there.

The war in El Salvador has gone on for years now, with no sign of peace in sight. Time and again it has seemed that the government has gained a decisive victory; but the guerrillas always crop out again, not much weaker than before. A point to be kept in mind vividly is that the leadership had roughly 8,000 troops when the war was started; today, though the losses in killed and captured have been considerable, they number more than 20,000.

Unsettling about this place in the North of Sri Lanka is not that one fears being molested—at any rate not during the day—but, rather, because of the sure knowledge that people of one's own sort, if suddenly faced with living this kind of life, would go under within three days. One feels very keenly that even a life like this has its own laws, and it would take years to learn them. A truck full of policemen: at once they scatter, some stand still and grin, while I look on and have no idea what is happening. Four boys and three girls are loaded into the truck, where they squat down among others who have already been picked up elsewhere. Indifferent, impenetrable. The police have helmets and automatics, therefore authority, but no knowledge. The newspapers carry a daily column of street attacks, sometimes naked corpses are discovered, and the murderers come as a rule from the other side. Whole districts without a single light. A landscape of brick hills, beneath them the buried, above them the twinkling stars; nothing stirs there but rats.

Reports from the Third World, the kind we read every morning over breakfast. The place-names are false, however. The locations involved are not Luanda and Beirut, El Salvador and Trincomalee; they are Rome and Frankfurt-am-Main, Athens and Berlin. Only forty-five years separate us from conditions we have become accustomed to thinking of as African, Asian or Latin American.

At the end of the Second World War, Europe was a pile of ruins, not only in a physical sense; it also seemed bankrupt in political and moral terms. It was not only the defeated Germans for whom the situation seemed hopeless. When Edmund Wilson came to London in July 1945, he found the English in a state of collective depression. The mood of the city reminded him of the cheerlessness of Moscow: 'How empty, how sickish, how senseless everything suddenly seems the moment the war is over! We are left flat with the impoverished and humiliating life that the drive against the enemy kept our minds off. Where our efforts have all gone toward destruction, we have been able to build nothing at home to fall back on amidst our own ruin.'

No one dared believe that the devastated continent could still have a future at all. As far as Europe was concerned, it seemed as if its history had come to an end with an overwhelming act of self-destruction, which the Germans had initiated and completed with savage energy: 'This is what exists,' noted Max Frisch in the spring of 1946, 'the grass growing in the houses, the dandelions in the churches and suddenly one can imagine how it might all continue to grow, how a forest might creep over our cities, slowly, inexorably, thriving unaided by human hands, a silence of thistles and moss, an earth without history, only the twittering of birds, spring, summer and autumn, the breathing of years, which there is no one to count any more.'

If, in the forties, someone had told the cave-dwellers of Dresden or Warsaw what life in 1990 would be like, they would have thought him crazy. But for people today, their own past has become just as unimaginable. They have long repressed and forgotten it, and those who are younger lack the imagination as well as the knowledge to make a picture of those distant times. It grows increasingly difficult, year by year, to imagine the condition of our continent at the end of the Second World War. The storytellers, apart from Heinrich Böll, Primo Levi, Hans Werner Richter, Louis-Ferdinand Céline and Curzio Malaparte and a few others, capitulated before the subject; the so-called *Trümmerliteratur*—literature of the ruins—hardly delivered what it promised.

Old newsreels show monotonous pictures of

destruction, the narration consists of hollow phrases; the films provide no indication of the inner state of the men and women passing through the devastated cities. The memoir literature that came later lacks authority, in part because the authors are often prone to self-justification and self-accusation. But another objection weighs more heavily, one which does not cast doubt on their integrity, but on their perspective. In looking back, they lose the very thing that should matter most: the coincidence of the observer with what he is looking at. The best sources tend to be the eyewitness accounts of contemporaries.

Studying eyewitness reports is, however, an odd experience. A peculiarity of the postwar period is a strange ignorance, a narrowing of horizons, that is unavoidable under extreme living conditions. At best it is a straightforward lack of knowledge of the world, which is easily explained by the years of isolation. John Gunther writes of a young soldier in Warsaw, with whom he entered into conversation on a summer evening in 1948: 'There was no nonsense about him. He knew exactly what Poland had suffered and what he himself had suffered. His ignorance of the outside world was, however, considerable. He had never met an American before. He wanted to know if New York had been made *kaputt* by the war like Warsaw.'

Elsewhere the Americans were looked at as though they were men from Mars, and everything they brought with them was treated with a reverence reminiscent of the cargo cults of Polynesia. During these years Europeans displayed attitudes akin to those found in the Third World. Someone who is only thinking of the next meal, who is forced to nail together a roof over his own head, will usually lack the desire and energy to make himself aware and well-informed. On top of that, there was the absence of freedom of movement. Millions were on the move, but only to save their skins. Travel, in the usual sense of the word, was not possible.

The poverty of sources is not, however, due to external causes alone. In the first years after the war, the long-term consequences of the Fascist dictatorships were becoming evident everywhere. That was true above all in Germany, but could also be observed elsewhere (there were collaborators in every occupied country). And this is exactly why those directly involved make the worst witnesses. Europeans took shelter behind a collective amnesia. Reality was not just ignored, it was flatly denied. With a mixture of lethargy, defiance and self-pity, they regressed to a kind of second childhood. Anyone meeting this syndrome for the first time was astonished; it seemed to be a form of moral insanity. When she visited the Rhineland in April 1945, the American journalist Martha Gellhorn was incensed, indeed staggered, by the statements of the Germans she met:

> No one is a Nazi. No one ever was. There may have been some Nazis in the next village, and as a matter of fact, that town about twenty kilometres away was a veritable hotbed of Nazidom. To tell you the truth, confidentially, there were a lot of Communists here. We were always known as very Red. Oh, the Jews? Well, there weren't really many Jews in this neighbourhood. Two, maybe six. They were taken away. I hid a Jew for six weeks. I hid a Jew for eight weeks. (I hid a Jew, he hid a Jew, all God's chillun hid Jews.) We have nothing

against the Jews; we always got on well with them. We have had enough of this government. Ah, how we have suffered. The bombs. We lived in the cellars for weeks. We welcome the Americans. We do not fear them; we have no reason to fear. We have done nothing wrong; we are not Nazis.

It should, we feel, be set to music. Then the Germans could sing this refrain and that would make it even better. They all talk like this. One asks oneself how the detested Nazi government, to which no one paid allegiance, managed to carry on this way for five and a half years. Obviously not a man, woman or child in Germany ever approved of the war for a minute, according to them. We stand around looking blank and contemptuous and listen to this story without friendliness and certainly without respect. To see a whole nation passing the buck is not an enlightening spectacle.

More than two years later, another observer from abroad, the journalist Janet Flanner, came to similar conclusions:

The new Germany is bitter against everyone else on earth, and curiously self-satisfied. Bursting with complaints of her hunger, lost homes, and other sufferings, she considers without interest or compassion the pains and losses she imposed on others, and she expects and takes, usually with carping rather than thanks, charity from those nations she tried to destroy . . . The significant Berlin catch-all phrase is: 'That was the war, but this is the peace.' This cryptic remark means, in free translation, that the people feel no responsibility for the war, which they regard as an act of history, and that they consider the troubles and confusions of the peace the Allies' fault. People here never mention Hitler's name any more. They just say darkly *'Früher war es besser'* (things were better before), meaning under Hitler. Only a few Germans seem to remember that, beginning with the occupations of 1940, some of them had the sense to launch the slogan 'Enjoy the war. The peace will be terrible.' It is.

So much for the state of consciousness of the Germans. Other Europeans were no less deluded. John Gunther reports: 'I asked one responsible Greek politician what the solution was, if any, and he replied in one word, "War". Indeed many conservative Greeks feel that nothing but outright war between the United States and the Soviet Union can rescue them; they actively want a war, horrible as this may seem, and make no bones about it. I asked my friend, "But do you think there is going to be a war?" He answered, "Europe is in anarchy. One hundred million people are slaves. We *have* to have war. There *must* be a war, or we will lose everything."'

Anyone who now turns to published opinion in the hope of gaining a clearer picture of the situation in postwar Europe, faces further disappointment. It is virtually impossible to find sober verdicts, intelligent analyses and convincing reportage in the newspaper and magazine columns of the years 1945 to 1948. That is not solely due to the restrictions imposed by the occupying powers. The state of mind of the journalists, their internal self-censorship is of much greater consequence. The Germans distinguished themselves in this respect too. Instead of coolly bearing witness to the facts, the intellectuals by and large took flight into abstractions. One searches in vain for the great reportage. What one finds, besides philosophical generalizations on the theme of collective guilt, are endless invocations of the Western tradition. Curious how much talk there is of Goethe, of humanism, the forgetfulness of being and the 'idea of freedom'. One gets the impression that this faded idealism is only another form of unconsciousness. Evidently it was not only the physical surroundings which were devastated, but the powers of observation as well. The whole of Europe had, as it were, 'been knocked on the head'.

For all of these reasons, little reliance can be placed on the testimony of those directly affected. Anyone who wants to get a reasonably accurate picture of conditions immediately after the war has to turn to other sources. There can be little doubt that our most trustworthy source is the gaze of the *outsider*. The most acute reports were provided by those authors who followed the victorious Allied armies. Among them stand out the best reporters of America, journalists such as Janet Flanner and Martha Gellhorn, and writers like Edmund Wilson, who did not think themselves too good to work for the press. They are all part of the great Anglo-Saxon tradition of literary reportage—continental Europeans have, until now, failed to produce anything to equal it. Other valuable sources were the product of chance, like the confidential reports of an American editor who worked for the US secret service, or the notes of émigrés who made the attempt to return to the Old World. Later, authors from countries which the war had spared, like the Swiss Max Frisch and the Swedish novelist Stig Dagerman, also made contributions.

They each came from a world which was similar to ours: orderly, normal, characterized by the thousand and one things we take for granted in a functioning civil society. The sense of shock engendered by the European disaster they confronted was all the greater. They could hardly believe their eyes in the face of the brutal, eccentric, terrifying and moving scenes, which they experienced in Paris and Naples, in the villages of Crete and the catacombs of Warsaw. It is the stranger's gaze which is able to make us comprehend what was happening in Europe then; for it does not rely on restrictive ideological analysis but on the telling physical detail. While the leading articles and polemics of the period have a strange mustiness about them, these eyewitness reports remain fresh.

The specialists in perception are at their best when they generalize least, when they do not censor the fantastic contradictions of the chaotic world they have entered, but leave them as they are. Max Frisch concludes his notes on Berlin quoted at the beginning with a laconic remark that silences all discussion of the state of civilization: 'A landscape of brick hills, beneath them the buried, above them the twinkling stars; nothing stirs there but rats. —Evening at the theatre: *Iphigenia.*'

An altogether startling degree of foresight emerges from the texts of these outsiders. In the capitals of the victorious powers at the time, whole planning commissions of politicians, economists and social scientists were at work, with the aim of writing reports on future developments in Europe. It is astonishing to discover that the accounts of the best journalists, who roamed the continent quite independently and relied only on their eyes and ears, are far superior to the analyses of these experts. A good example is Martha Gellhorn's reportage of July 1944, a time when not a soul in Washington was thinking about the Cold War. In a village on the Adriatic, in the middle of an artillery duel, Gellhorn got into conversation with soldiers of a Polish unit fighting against the Germans:

> They had come a long way from Poland. They call themselves the Carpathian Lancers because most of them escaped from Poland over the Carpathian mountains. They had been gone from their country for almost five years. For three and a half years this cavalry regiment, which was formed in Syria, fought in the Middle East and the Western Desert. Last January they returned to their own continent of Europe, via Italy, and it was the Polish Corps, with this armoured regiment fighting in it as infantry, that finally took Cassino in May. In June they started their great drive up the Adriatic, and the prize, Ancona—which this regiment had entered first—lay behind us.
>
> It is a long road home to Poland, to the great Carpathian mountains, and every mile of road has been bought most bravely. But now they do not know what they are going home to.

They fight an enemy in front of them and fight him superbly. And with their whole hearts they fear an ally, who is already in their homeland. For they do not believe that Russia will relinquish their country after the war; they fear that they are to be sacrificed in this peace, as Czechoslovakia was in 1938. It must be remembered that almost every one of these men, irrespective of rank, class or economic condition, has spent time in either a German or a Russian prison during this war. It must be remembered that for five years they have had no news from their families, many of whom are still prisoners in Russia or Germany. It must be remembered that these Poles have only twenty-one years of national freedom behind them, and a long aching memory of foreign rule.

So we talked of Russia and I tried to tell them that their fears must be wrong or there would be no peace in the world. That Russia must be as great in peace as she has been in war, and that the world must honour the valour and suffering of the Poles by giving them freedom to rebuild and better their homeland. I tried to say I could not believe that this war, which is fought to maintain the rights of man, will end by ignoring the rights of Poles. But I am not a Pole; I belong to a large free country and I speak with the optimism of those who are forever safe. And I remember the tall, gentle twenty-two-year-old soldier who drove me in a Jeep one day, and how quietly he explained that his father had died of hunger in a German prison camp, and his mother and sister had been silent for four years in a labour camp in Russia, and his brother was missing, and he had no profession because he had entered the army when he was seventeen and so had had no time to learn anything. Remembering this boy, and all the others I knew, with their appalling stories of hardship and homelessness, it seemed to me that no American had the right to talk to the Poles, since we had never even brushed such suffering ourselves.

The editors of *Collier's* magazine, for which Martha Gellhorn was working, refused to publish this report, because the Poles' prophetic remarks about the Soviet Union, the United States' most important ally, did not suit them.

What makes the work of these reporters so illuminating is not that they lay claim to a higher objectivity, but the reverse, that they hold on to their radically subjective viewpoint, even when—especially when—they put themselves in the wrong. Among the costs of immediacy is that one is infected by one's surroundings and cannot stand above them. The sore points in the context of the postwar years emerge all the more clearly; the frictions between English and Americans, the fury of the victors at the grandiose impudence of the Italians, above all the hatred of the Germans, which in some observers turns to disgust and a desire for revenge. Whoever had behaved like the Germans and whoever continued to behave like them—that is, without any remorse—could not expect *fairness*; almost all representatives of the victorious nations were convinced of that, and it is by no means superfluous to be reminded of the extreme expressions of feeling during those years.

It is not surprising that the observers from neutral countries are more sophisticated in their judgements. Not that one could accuse them of particular sympathies for the Germans; but they are more able than the victors to recognize the ambiguities of their own role. After a visit to Germany in autumn 1946, the Swede Stig Dagerman wrote:

> If any commentary is to be risked on the mood of bitterness towards the Allies, mixed with self-contempt, with apathy, with comparisons to the disadvantage of the present—all of which were certain to strike the visitor that gloomy autumn—it is necessary to keep in mind a whole series of particular occurrences and physical conditions. It is important to remember that statements implying dissatisfaction with, or even distrust of, the goodwill of the victorious democracies were made not in an airless room or on a theatrical stage echoing with ideological repartee, but in all too palpable cellars in Essen, Hamburg or Frankfurt-am-Main. Our autumn picture of the family in the waterlogged cellar also contains a journalist who, carefully balancing on planks set across the water, interviews the family on their views of the newly constituted democracy in their country, asks them about their hopes and illusions, and, above all, asks if the family was better off under Hitler. The answer that the visitor then receives has this result: stooping with rage, nausea and contempt,

the journalist scrambles hastily backwards out of
the stinking room, jumps into his hired English
car or American Jeep, and half an hour later over
a drink or a good glass of real German beer, in
the bar of the press hotel composes a report on
the subject 'Nazism is alive in Germany'.

Fifty years after the catastrophe Europe understands
itself more than ever as a common project, yet it is far
from achieving a comprehensive analysis of its
beginnings in the years immediately following the
Second World War. The memory of the period is
incomplete and provincial, insofar as it has not entirely
given way to repression or nostalgia. That is not only
because people were busy with their own survival and
hardly bothered with what was happening next door; it
is also because now they are reluctant to talk about the
skeletons in the cupboard. We prefer to address the
glowing future of the European Community or the
opening up of Eastern Europe, rather than think about
those unpleasant times, when no one would have put a
brass farthing on a rebirth of our continent. A somewhat
fatal strategy, for in retrospect it appears that during the
years 1944–48, without the protagonists suspecting it,
the seeds were sown, not only of future successes but also
of future conflicts.

A high-explosive bomb is a high-explosive bomb, a
hunger swelling does not distinguish between black and
white, just and unjust, but neither the destructive power
of the air forces, nor the postwar misery was capable of
homogenizing Europe and extinguishing its differences.
These differences were not visible in the burnt earth, but
had hibernated in people's heads. The European societies

were like cities that had been destroyed, but for which detailed construction diagrams and land registers had been preserved; their invisible circuit and critical path diagrams and network plans had survived the destruction, and in all their variety. Differences in traditions, capacities, mentalities re-emerged. Attempts at resuscitation were correspondingly diverse.

As Norman Lewis wrote in his Naples reportage of 1944:

It is astonishing to witness the struggles of this city so shattered, so starved, so deprived of all those things that justify a city's existence, to adapt itself to a collapse into conditions which must resemble life in the Dark Ages. People camp out like Bedouins in deserts of brick. There is little food, little water, no salt, no soap. A lot of Neapolitans have lost their possessions, including most of their clothing, in the bombings, and I have seen some strange combinations of garments about the streets, including a man in an old dinner-jacket, knickerbockers and army boots, and several women in lacy confections that might have been made up from curtains. There are no cars but carts by the hundred, and a few antique coaches such as barouches and phaetons drawn by lean horses. Today at Posilippo I stopped to watch the methodical dismemberment of a stranded German half-track by a number of youths who were streaming away from it like leaf-cutter ants, carrying pieces of metal in all shapes and sizes. Fifty yards away a well-dressed lady with a feather in her hat squatted to milk a goat. At the water's edge below, two fishermen had roped together several doors salvaged from the ruins, piled their gear on these and were about to go fishing. Inexplicably no boats are allowed out, but nothing is said in the proclamation about rafts. Everyone improvises and adapts.

The attitudes that Lewis describes have remained characteristic of the population of southern Italy up to the present day: an ingenuity which knows how to take advantage of every opening, a parasitism of quite heroic energy and an untiring readiness to exploit a hostile world. At about the same time, the priorities of the French were quite different. In February 1945, Janet Flanner wrote:

The brightest news here is the infinite resilience of the French as human beings. Parisians are politer and more patient in their troubles than they were in their prosperity. Though they have no soap that lathers, both men and women smell civilized when you encounter them in the Métro, which everybody rides in, there being no buses or taxis. Everything here is a substitute for something else. The women who are not neat, thin and frayed look neat, thin and chic clattering along in their platform shoes of wood—substitute for shoe leather—which sound like horses' hoofs. Their broad-shouldered, slightly shabby coats of sheepskin—substitute for wool cloth which the Nazis preferred for themselves—were bought on the black market three winters ago. The Paris *midinettes*, for whom, because of their changeless gaiety, there is really no substitute on earth . . . still wear their home-made, fantastically high, upholstered Charles X turbans. Men's trousers are shabby, since they are not something that can be run up at home. The young intellectuals of both sexes go about in ski clothes. This is what the resistance wore when it was fighting and freezing outdoors in the *maquis*, and it has set the Sorbonne undergraduate style.

The more serious normalities of traditional Paris life go on in readjusted form. Candy shops display invitations to come in and register for your sugar almonds, the conventional sweet for French baptisms, but you must have a doctor's certificate swearing that you and your wife are really expecting. Giddy, young wedding parties that can afford the price pack off to the wedding luncheon two by two in *vélo-taxis*, bicycle-barouches which are hired for hundreds of francs an hour. The other evening your correspondent saw a more modest bridal couple starting off on their life journey together in the Métro. They stood apart from everyone else on the Odéon platform, the groom in his rented *smoking* and with a *boutonnière*, the bride all in white—that is, a white raincoat, white rubber boots, white sweater and skirt, white turban, and a large, old-fashioned white nosegay. They were holding hands. American soldiers across the tracks shouted good wishes to them.

Of course such descriptions also express the

prejudices and *idées reçues* of the particular observer. But such an interpretation misses the point. That is especially clear from the following report by John Gunther. It flies in the face of just about every cliché about the Poles.

> This concentrated tornado of pure useless horror turned Warsaw into Pompeii. I heard a serious-minded Pole say, 'Perhaps a few cats may have been alive, but certainly not a dog.' After liberation early in 1945 the Polish government took the heroic decision to rebuild.
>
> Every Pole I met was almost violent with hope. 'See that?' A cabinet minister pointed to something that looked like a smashed gully. 'In twenty years that will be our Champs Elysées.'
>
> Particularly impressive is [the work of rebuilding] in the Old City, which is almost as complete a ruin as the ghetto. A patch of ravaged brick is all that remains of the Angelski Hotel where Napoleon stayed. The old bricks are used in the new structures, which gives a crazy patchwork effect. Hundreds of houses are only half rebuilt; as soon as a single room is habitable, people move in. I never saw anything more striking than the way a few pieces of timber shore up a shattered heap of stone or brick, so that a kind of perch-like room or nest is made available to a family, high over crumbling ruins. One end of a small building may be a pile of dust; at the other end you will see curtains in the windows.
>
> Much of this furious reconstruction is done

by voluntary labour; most, moreover, is done by human hand. Even cabinet ministers go out and work on Sunday. In all Warsaw, there are not more than two or three concrete mixers and three or four electric hoists; in all Warsaw, not one bulldozer! A gang of men climb up a wall, fix an iron hook on the end of a rope to the topmost bricks, climb down and pull. Presto!— the wall crashes. Then some distorted bricks go into what is going up. The effect is almost like that of double exposure in a film. No time for correct masonry!

So this catastrophically gutted city, probably the most savage ruin ever made by the hand of evil mankind anywhere, is being transformed into a new metropolis boiling and churning with vigour. Brick by brick, minute by minute, hand by hand, Warsaw is being made to live again through the fixed creative energy and imagination of immensely gifted and devoted people.

Quite different feelings were aroused in another visitor who observed the beginnings of German reconstruction on a journey through southern Germany. One will hardly be able to argue that Alfred Döblin's comments have lost any of their force in the course of the past decades.

A principal impression made by the country, and it provokes the greatest astonishment in someone arriving at the end of 1945, is that the people are running back and forward in the ruins like ants whose nest has been destroyed.

Agitated and eager to work, their major grievance is that they cannot set to immediately, for the lack of materials, the lack of directions.

The destruction does not make them depressed, but acts as an intense stimulus to work. I am convinced that if they had the means that they lack, they would rejoice, only rejoice, that their old, out-of-date, badly planned towns have been destroyed, and that now they had been given the opportunity to put down something first class, altogether modern.

A populous town such as Stuttgart: crowds of people, their number further increased by an influx of refugees from other cities and regions, went about the streets among the dreadful ruins truly as if nothing had happened and as if the city had always looked as it does now. At any rate, the sight of the wrecked houses had no effect on them.

And if anyone believes, or once believed, that misfortune in one's own land and the sight of such devastation would cause people to think and have an educative effect on them—then he can see for himself that he was mistaken. People point out certain groups of houses, saying: 'Those were hit during this bombing and the others were hit during that bombing,' and tell a few anecdotes. And that's all. No particular message follows, and there are certainly no further reflections. People go to their work, stand in queues here, as everywhere else, for food.

Already there are theatres, concerts and

cinemas here and there, and all apparently are well attended. The trams are running, horribly crowded as they are everywhere. People are practical and help one another. They are concerned with the immediate present in a way that is already troubling the thoughtful.

Here lives, as before, an industrious, orderly people. They have always obeyed the government. They obeyed Hitler too, and by and large do not grasp why this time obedience is supposed to have been bad. It will be much easier to rebuild their cities than to get them to comprehend what it was they have experienced and to understand how it all happened.

It may appear unjust that the verdict on the reconstruction efforts of the people of Stuttgart turns out so ill-humouredly in comparison with the praise bestowed on those of Warsaw. But one cannot understand the puzzling energy of the Germans, if one resists the idea that they have turned their defects into virtues. Insensibility proved to be the condition of their future success. The tricky quality of this relationship emerges from the following report by Robert Thompson Pell, an American secret service officer, who, in the spring of 1945, was faced with the task of examining the activities during the Third Reich of the top managers of the I.G. Farben company.

> On the whole I gained the impression that the German leaders had gone over to accommodating themselves to necessity—but only to a limited extent. In the meanwhile, they are sounding out our weak points, putting us to the

test at every opportunity, trying to find out if we really mean it when we thump the table, and offering as much resistance as they dare. They say almost openly that we will not be able to cope with the situation ourselves and will have to turn to them again in the end. They are relying on us to make so many mistakes that it will be inevitable that they take charge again. Till then they will bide their time and look on, while we bungle everything. Apart from that, they play up the 'red peril' as much as they dare. As soon as one shows oneself to be even a little approachable—or if they believe they can see signs of it—they tell us again and again: 'We are so glad that you are here and not the Russians,' and in a few cases they've actually maintained that the German army withdrew so that we could save as much of West Germany from the Russians as could be saved.

The directors whom I fetched in my Jeep every day were itching to tell me that the German people had been the victim of a worldwide conspiracy that had intended to deliver up this lovely country to unknown forces; Germany had conducted a defensive war; the Allied 'terror raids' had united the German people, had no military value and had been a serious error; they were the true defenders of Western civilization against 'the Asiatic hordes'.

In short, the country was in chaos and the people were in a hysterical condition which quickly grew into an attitude of defiance and a feeling of being treated unjustly, and which was not clouded by the least trace of guilt. Most of these men of high, in some cases the highest, standing in society were ready to admit that Germany had lost the war, but were quick to add the reason was the superiority of the Allies in power and material; they then immediately added that in future they would try to make that good. The overall impression was, in short, disquieting. So far as I could ascertain, the attitude of the average manager was characterized by self-pity, fawning self-justification and an injured sense of innocence, which was accompanied by a yammering for pity and for aid in the reconstruction of his devastated country. Many of them, if not the majority, confidently expect that American capital will commit itself without delay to the work of reconstruction, and they declared themselves ready to place their labour power and their intellect at the service of these temporary masters; as a consequence they openly expect to rebuild a Germany more powerful and bigger than it was in the past.

Thanks to the irony of history or, rather, its mockery, these delusions of 1945 have, in a way, become reality. That those who were defeated then, the Germans and the Japanese, today feel like victors, is more than a moral scandal; it is a political provocation. Our leaders naturally never tire of protesting that in the meantime we have all become peaceable, democratic and moderate; in a word, well-behaved. The most remarkable thing about this assertion is that it is true. This mutation has turned the Germans into what they once accused others of being: a nation of shopkeepers. In that, they are by no means alone. All the nations of Europe are, with varying success, trying to do the same. Since the end of the Communist monopoly of power, the primacy of economics also appears to be establishing itself in the eastern part of the continent. Fifty years after the Second World War, this much is certain: not only did the German suicide attempt fail, but that of Europe as a whole. The more, however, our continent moves back into the centre of world politics and of the world market, the more a new kind of Eurocentrism will gain ground. A slogan copyrighted by none other than Joseph Goebbels has reappeared in public debate: 'Fortress Europe'. It once had a military meaning; it returns as an economic and demographic concept. Under these circumstances a booming Europe will do well to remind itself of a Europe in ruins, from which it is separated by only a few decades.

THE GREAT MIGRATION

THIRTY-THREE SIGNPOSTS

With a footnote
'Concerning Certain Peculiarities of the Manhunt'

We no longer know whom we should esteem and honour. In this regard we have become as Barbarians to one another. For by nature we are all equal, whether we are Barbarians or Greeks. That follows from what by nature is indispensable to all men. We all breathe through the mouth and nose, and we all eat with our hands.

Antiphon, 'Of Truth'. Fifth century BC.

By the Statue of Liberty is the inscription: 'In this republican land all men are born free and equal.' But under it in tiny characters stands: 'Excepting the tribe of Hamo.'—That nullifies the other. Ah ye republicans!

Herman Melville, 'Mardi and a voyage thither'. 1849.

I

A MAP of the world. Swarms of blue and red arrows condense into eddies before scattering in opposite directions again. Underlying this diagram are curves which demarcate the colour-tinted zones of varying air pressure, isobars and winds. Such a weather chart looks pretty, but it cannot be accurately interpreted without previous knowledge. It is abstract. It has to represent a dynamic process by static means. Only a film could show what is really going on. The normal state of the atmosphere is turbulence. The same is true of the settlement of the earth by human beings.

II

EVEN AFTER more than a century of research into the Palaeolithic, the origin of *Homo sapiens* has still not been resolved beyond doubt. It seems agreed, however, that the species first appeared on the African continent and that it spread over the whole planet, in complicated and perilous stages, by way of a long chain of migrations. Staying put is not one of our species' genetically fixed characteristics; it developed relatively late and is probably connected with the invention of cultivation. Our primary existence is that of hunters, collectors and shepherds.

Certain atavistic features of our behaviour which otherwise seem puzzling, such as mass tourism or the passionate love of the car, may be explained by this nomadic past.

III

THE CONFLICT between nomadic and settled tribes is made manifest in the myth of Cain and Abel: 'And Abel was a keeper of sheep, but Cain was a tiller of the ground.' The territorial conflict ends in murder. The point of the story is that the farmer, after he has killed the nomad, is dispossessed in turn: 'A fugitive and a vagabond shalt thou be on the earth.'

The history of humanity can be read as the unfolding of this parable. Stationary populations form again and again over the millennia. On the whole, however, they remain the exception. The rule is: conquest and pillage, expulsion and exile, slavery and abduction, colonization and captivity. A considerable proportion of humanity has always been in motion, migrating or in flight for the most diverse reasons, in a violent or peaceful manner—a circulation which must lead to perpetual turbulence. It is a chaotic process which frustrates every attempt at planning, every long-term forecast.

IV

TWO PASSENGERS in a railway compartment. We know nothing about them, their origin or their destination. They have made themselves at home and have commandeered the little tables, coat-hooks and baggage-racks. Newspapers, coats and bags lie around on the empty seats. The door opens and two new travellers enter. Their arrival is not welcomed. A distinct reluctance to move up, to clear the free seats and let the newcomers share them is evident. The original passengers, even if they do not know one another, behave with a remarkable degree of solidarity. They display a united front against the new arrivals. The compartment has become their territory, and they regard each new arrival as an intruder. Their consciousness is that of natives claiming the whole space for themselves. This view cannot be rationally justified. It appears all the more deeply rooted.

Nevertheless, matters rarely get to the point of open conflict. The passengers are subject to a system of rules that is not dependent on them. Their territorial instinct is curbed both by the institutional code of the railroad and by other unwritten norms of behaviour such as courtesy. So only looks are exchanged and formulaic apologies muttered through clenched teeth. The new passengers are tolerated. One gets used to them. Yet they remain, even to a diminishing degree, stigmatized.

This harmless model is not without its absurd features. The railway compartment is itself a transitory domicile, a location which serves only to change locations. Fluctuation is its nature. The passenger is the negation of the sedentary person. He has traded a real territory for a virtual one. Despite this, he defends his transient abode with sullen resentment.

V

EVERY MIGRATION, no matter what triggered it, what motive underlies it, whether it is voluntary or involuntary, and what scale it assumes, leads to conflicts. Sectional self-interest and xenophobia are anthropological constants which predate every rationalization. Their universal distribution indicates that they are older than all known societies.

In order to check them, to avoid blood baths and to make possible even a minimum of exchange and communication between different clans, tribes and ethnic groups, ancient societies invented the taboos and rituals of hospitality. These provisions, however, do not abrogate the status of the stranger. Quite the reverse: they fix it. The guest is sacred, but he must not stay.

VI

TWO NEW passengers open the compartment door. From this instant, the status of those who entered earlier changes. Only a moment ago, they were the intruders; now, all at once, they are natives. They belong to the sedentary clan of compartment-occupants and claim all the privileges the latter believe are due to them. The defence of an 'ancestral' territory that was only recently occupied appears paradoxical. The occupants do not empathize with the newcomers, who have to struggle against the same opposition and face the same difficult initiation which they recently underwent. Curious, the rapidity with which one's own origin is concealed and denied.

VII

CLAN AND tribal groups have existed since the earth was inhabited by human beings; nations have existed for only 200 years or so. It is not difficult to see the difference. Ethnic groups come into being semi-spontaneously, 'of their own accord'; nations are consciously created, and are often artificial entities, which cannot get by without a specific ideology. This ideological foundation, together with its rituals and emblems (flags, anthems), originated in the nineteenth century. From Europe and North America, it has spread over the whole world.

A country that wants to succeed as a nation needs a well-coded self-consciousness, its own system of institutions (army, customs and excise, police, diplomatic corps) and numerous legal means of demarcating itself externally (sovereignty, citizenship, passports). Some, but not all, nations have been successful in transferring older forms of identification on to themselves. That is a difficult operation psychologically, for powerful feelings which once inspired smaller associations have to be mobilized on behalf of modern state formations. It is rarely achieved without historical legends. If necessary, proof of a glorious past is forged, venerable traditions simply invented. The abstract idea of the nation, however, could only acquire an independent life where the state was able to develop organically out of more ancient conditions. The more artificial a nation's genesis, the more precarious and hysterical its national feeling. That holds true for the 'over-due nations' of Europe, for the new states that emerged from the colonial system, as well as for forced unions like the former Soviet Union and Yugoslavia, which have a tendency towards disintegration and civil war.

Of course, no nation has an absolutely homogenous ethnic population. This fact is in fundamental conflict with the national feeling that has taken shape in most states. As a rule, the leading national group consequently finds it difficult to reconcile itself to the existence of minorities, and every wave of immigrants is considered a political problem. The most important exceptions to this pattern are those modern states which owe their existence to migration on a large scale; above all the United States, Canada and Australia. Their founding myth is the *tabula rasa*. The reverse of this coin is the extermination of the indigenous population, whose remnants have only very recently been conceded essential minority rights.

Almost all other nations justify their existence by a firm self-ascription. The distinction between 'our own' people and 'strangers' appears quite natural to them, even if it is questionable historically. Whoever wishes to hold on to the distinction would need to maintain, according to his own logic, that he has always been there—a thesis which can all too easily be disproved. To that extent, a proper national history assumes the ability to forget everything that doesn't fit.

However, it is not only one's own motley origin that is denied. Movements of migration on a large scale always lead to struggles over the distribution of resources. National feeling prefers to reinterpret these inevitable conflicts as though the dispute had more to do with imaginary than with material resources. The struggle is then over the difference between self- and external ascriptions, a field that offers demagogy ideal possibilities for development.

EXTERNAL AND self-ascription can never be made to coincide. That's inevitable. Their harmonious correspondence is always an apparent one. The sentence 'The Finns are cunning and drunken' means something quite different depending on whether a Finn or a Swede is speaking. Consider the different reactions it provokes. Among Finns only a Finn is allowed to say it; coming from a Swede it would be scandalous.

Such differences always conceal a long history of contact and conflict. The interaction between self- and external ascriptions is complicated. Curiosity and integration, defensiveness and a sense of injury, resentment and projection play a part, as do strategies of self-criticism, of irony and the allaying of suspicion.

Originally, however, things were very simple:

The Nahua Indians called the neighbouring tribes *popolaca*, which means 'stammerers', and *mazahua*, 'those who bellow like stags'.

In Russian, a German is called *nemets*; this word is derived from *nemoi* which means 'dumb'—that is, someone who cannot speak. The Greek word *barbaros* for non-Greeks initially had the meaning 'stammering' or 'babbling' and often implies 'uneducated', 'vulgar', 'cowardly', 'cruel', 'uncultured', 'violent', 'avaricious' and 'treacherous'.

The Hottentots, a word that in Afrikaans means 'stutterer', call themselves *k'oi-n*, 'the human beings'.

For the Ainu too, the group name is identical to the word for human being, whereas the Japanese call them *emishi*, 'barbarians'.

The same is true of the Kamchatkans—who describe themselves as *itelmen*—'human beings', and outdone only by the Chukchi who maintain that they are *luo-rovetlan*, that is 'the true human beings'.

Claude Lévi-Strauss has described this universally diffused self-awareness as follows:

'It is well known that the concept "mankind" which includes all life-patterns of the species man, without distinction of race or civilizations, arose very late and is not widespread . . . Mankind stops at the boundaries of the tribe, the linguistic group, sometimes even of the village, so that a large number of so-called primitive peoples give themselves a name which means "men" (or sometimes "the good", "the excellent" or "the perfect") which simultaneously indicates that the other tribes, groups or villages have no share in the good qualities—or even in the nature—of man but, at most, consist of the "the bad", "the evil", "ground apes" or "lice eggs". Sometimes the strangers are even denied this last foothold in reality, and are regarded as "phantoms" or "apparitions". There arises the curious situation of two interlocutors remorselessly trading their derogatory epithets.'

IX

CONTEMPORARY MIGRATIONS differ from earlier movements of people in more than one respect. First, mobility has increased enormously in the past two centuries. European oceanic trade first created the capacity which made possible the movement of millions over great distances. The developed world market requires global mobilization and imposes it by force where necessary, as with the opening of Japan and China in the nineteenth century. Capital tears down national barriers. It can make tactical use of patriotic and racist impulses, but disregards them strategically because the commercial interest can have no particular concerns. The free movement of capital tends to draw that of labour behind it, without regard for race or nationality. With the globalization of the world market (which was completed only very recently), the new migratory movements will also achieve a new quality. Molecular mass movements will presumably take the place of state-organized colonial wars, expeditions of conquest and expulsions. Whereas electronic money follows only its own logic and playfully overcomes every resistance, human beings act as if they were subject to some incomprehensible compulsion. Their embarkations are like movements of flight, which it would be cynical to call voluntary.

X

NO ONE emigrates without the promise of something better. In earlier times, legend and rumour were the media of hope. The Promised Land, Arabia Felix, legendary Atlantis, El Dorado, the New World; these were the magical stories that motivated many to set out. Today it is the high-frequency images which the global media system transmits to the very last village of the poor world. Their reality content is even less than that of the marvellous legends of the early modern period; however, their effects are incomparably more powerful. Advertising, especially, which is effortlessly understood in its wealthy countries of origin as a mere sign without real referents, counts in the Second and Third Worlds as a reliable description of a possible way of life. To a large extent it determines the horizon of expectations which are associated with emigration.

XI

FOR CENTURIES the exchange of population was almost a zero-sum game. The world's population displayed fluctuations over space and time, but the absolute increase was so insignificant that it hardly mattered. However, since it has begun to grow exponentially, the rules of the game have changed. Sooner or later the unimaginable quantitative increase must have an effect on the quality of the migratory movements.

That this is already the case is doubtful. Today it is estimated that more than twenty million immigrants from other zones live in Western Europe. The flow of refugees in Africa and Asia is on a similar scale. These are large numbers. But if one considers that between 1810 and 1921 thirty-four million people, mainly from Europe, emigrated to the United States alone, then it is hardly possible to argue that these figures are beyond historical comparison. Indeed, migration has, so far, been rather limited, especially if measured against the absolute increase in the world's population (the United Nations forecasts a growth of almost one billion for 1990–2000). This invites the conclusion that only a fraction of the potential migrants has actually set itself in motion: the real migration of peoples is still to come.

The media anticipate this future prospect in a dangerous fashion, and describe it in quite fantastic terms. A strange enjoyment of fear emerges from the apocalyptic pictures they project. All the present-day phenomena of crisis—the unstable condition of the world economy, the huge technological dangers, the disintegration of the Soviet empire, the ecological threat—provoke scenarios of this kind. The anticipatory panic may even serve as immunization, a kind of psychic inoculation. At any rate it leads not to attempts to find solutions but, at best, to stop-go policies, alternating between timid repair measures and blocks on thought and action.

XII

A LIFEBOAT is packed with survivors from a shipwreck. In the stormy sea around it there are other people in danger of going under. How should the occupants of the boat behave? Should they push away or hack off the hands of the next person who grabs the side of the boat? That would be murder. Pull him on? Then the boat would sink taking all the survivors with it. The dilemma is part of the standard repertoire of casuistry. The moral philosophers and all the rest who discuss it usually pay no attention to the fact that they themselves are safely on dry land. Yet all abstract reflections founder on just this 'as if', no matter what their conclusion. The best intention is frustrated by the cosiness of the seminar room, because no one can credibly declare how he would behave in an emergency.

The parable of the lifeboat is reminiscent of the railway-compartment scenario. It is that model taken to its extreme. Here, also, travellers act as if they were property owners, with the difference that the ancestral territory they are defending is a drifting nutshell, and that it is no longer a matter of a little more comfort, but of life and death.

It is, of course, no accident that the image of the lifeboat recurs in the political discourse about immigration, usually in the form of the assertion, 'The boat is full.' That this sentence is factually inaccurate is the least that can be said about it. A look around is enough to disprove it. Those who make use of it know that too. They are not interested in its truthfulness, however, but in the illusion it conjures up, and that is an astonishing one. Evidently many West Europeans believe that their lives are in danger. They compare their situation with that of shipwreck survivors. The metaphor is turned upside-down, as it were. Suddenly those who have a roof over their heads imagine that they are fleeing *boat people*, emigrants sailing steerage, Albanians on an overcrowded ghost ship. The distress at sea which is hallucinated in this way is presumably intended to justify behaviour which is only conceivable in extreme situations. From here it is not a very big step to the hacked-off hands in the parable.

XIII

THERE IS something comforting about the railway-compartment analogy, simply because the scene of the action is so restricted. Even in the terrifying image of the life-boat, individual human beings can still be recognized—as in Géricault's painting, *The Raft of the 'Medusa'*, where eighteen faces, actions, fates, can be distinguished. Contemporary statistics, whether referring to the starving, the unemployed or refugees, express everything in millions. Such numbers paralyse the imagination. The aid organizations and their campaign managers know that too, which is why they always show just one child with huge, pathetic eyes, so as to make the catastrophe commensurate with our compassion. But the terror of the big number is without eyes. Empathy breaks down before such excessive demand, and reason is made aware of its impotence.

XIV

SUPERFLUOUS, SUPERFLUOUS . . . an excellent word I've come up with. The deeper I plunge into myself and the closer I examine the whole of my past life, the more I am convinced of the harsh truth of that expression. Superfluous—precisely so. The word does not apply to other people . . . People are good and evil, intelligent and stupid, pleasant and unpleasant; but superfluous?

It would not have occurred to Ivan Turgenev to regard the peasants on his estate, still less whole villages, regions, peoples, continents as superfluous. Although his hero Chulkaturin, in the novel *Diary of a Superfluous Man* (whose situation seems almost idyllic 150 years after his demise), talks in such terms of his landowning father with his country houses, and of himself—his boredom, his loneliness and his disgust—'The word does not apply to other people,' he thinks.

But he has been proved mistaken. Of course there have been great massacres and endemic poverty in every age. Enemies were enemies, and the poor were poor; yet only since history has become world history have whole peoples seen themselves condemned to superfluousness, and that by authors who remain strangely subjectless. The judges who pass this sentence go under the names of 'colonialism', 'industrialization', 'technological progress', 'revolution', 'collectivization', 'final solution', 'Versailles' or 'Yalta', and their decrees are pronounced openly and put into practice systematically, so that no one can be in any doubt what fate is intended for him: flight from the land or emigration, expulsion or genocide.

State-organized crime continues to be widespread. The overarching, anonymous world market, however, appears ever more clearly as the instance which condemns increasingly large sections of mankind to superfluousness. It does so not through political persecution, by command of the Führer or party resolution, but spontaneously, by its own logic, so that more and more people fall out of it. The result is no less murderous, but the guilty are even less likely to be brought to book than before. In the language of economics that means: an enormously increasing supply of human beings is faced with a declining demand. Even in wealthy societies people are rendered superfluous daily. What should be done with them?

XV

THE LOGICAL status of hallucinations is such that two mutually exclusive phobias can find room in the same brain without any problem at all. So it is that many supporters of the lifeboat model are simultaneously obsessed with a delusion which expresses precisely the opposite fear. Again an assertion of the facts is proffered: 'The Germans (French, Swedes, Italians) are dying out.' Long-term extrapolations of current population statistics are produced to serve as the basis for these slogans, even though such forecasts have repeatedly proved mistaken in the past; scenarios illustrate the terrible conse-quences—an ageing population, decadence, depopula-tion—accompanied by concerned glances at economic growth, tax revenue and the pension system.

The idea that too many and too few people could simultaneously exist in the same territory causes panic—an affliction for which the term *demographic bulimia* might be appropriate.

XVI

ANALYSES FROM those far-off times when an attempt was made to advance a political economy of migration appear comforting in their sobriety compared with the delirious ramblings of the present day. At the turn of the century the American economist Richmond Mayo Smith offered a model example of such cool-headed reflection:

> The amount of money brought by the immig-rants is not large, and is probably more than off-set by the money sent back by immigrants for the support of families and friends at home or to aid them in following. The valuable element is the able-bodied immigrant himself as a factor of production. It is said, for instance, that an adult slave used to be valued at between $800 and $1,000, so that every adult immigrant may be looked upon as worth that sum to the

country. Or it has been said that an adult immigrant represents what it would cost to bring up a child from infancy, to the age, say, of fifteen. This has been estimated by Ernst Engel as amounting to $550 for a German child. The most scientific procedure, however, is to calculate the probable earnings of the immigrant during the rest of his 'lifetime', and deduct these from his expenses of living. The remainder represents his net earnings which he will contribute to the well-being of the new country. W. Farr reckoned this to be, in the case of unskilled English emigrants, about £175. Multiplying the total number of adult immigrants, we get the annual value of immigration. Such attempts to put a precise money value on immigration are futile. They neglect the question of quality and of opportunity. The immigrant is worth what it has cost to bring him up only if he is able-bodied, honest and willing to work. If he is diseased, crippled, dishonest or indolent, he may be a direct loss to the community instead of a gain. So, too, the immigrant is worth his future net earnings to the community only if there is a demand for his labour.

XVII

FOR A long time there was greater anxiety in Europe about the consequences of emigration than of immigration. This debate stretches back into the eighteenth century. The concept of population as wealth derives from the theories of mercantilism. In those days emigration was regarded as a haemorrhage, and the attempt was made to limit, even forbid it. Secret emigration, particularly recruitment for and the abetting of emigration, was subject to severe punishment in many states, a practice which communist states adhered to until very recently. Louis XIV had the French borders carefully watched in order to keep his subjects in the land, and in England there was a ban on the emigration of qualified artisans until the middle of the nineteenth century. The so-called Free or Departure Money, an emigration tax imposed on the estates of emigrants, was in force in Germany until 1817, and the Nazis reverted to this confiscatory procedure when they did not yet want to murder the Jews, only expel them.

XVIII

IRELAND IS the classic example of a country of emigration. Brutal exploitation by the English led, in the 1840s, to a catastrophic famine, from which the country has never fully recovered. In 1843 Ireland had a population of eight and a half million; in 1961 this figure had fallen to less than three million. In the period from 1851 to 1901 an average of seventy-two per cent of all Irish people emigrated. Ireland remains one of the poorest countries in Western Europe. One can endlessly debate whether emigration is to blame for its poverty, or whether, on the contrary, it improved the situation of the inhabitants.

A naïve but illuminating conclusion is drawn by the anonymous contributor to a lexicon dating from 1843:

Emigration is weak as a remedy against pauperism. If today one could remove all the poor from the lands visited by pauperism, then there would be, should its causes continue to be active, just as many again in twenty years, perhaps in ten . . . In the main the state should strive to establish and maintain such conditions within its borders, so that at least destitution and dissatisfaction do not drive the people forth.

XIX

EMIGRANTS NEVER represent a cross-section of the whole population, a fact which is of crucial importance to any estimation of the consequences. 'It is the man of energy, of some means, of ambition, who takes the chances of success in the new country, leaving the poor, the indolent, the weak and crippled at home,' wrote Mayo Smith. 'It is maintained that such emigration institutes a process of selection which is not favourable to the home country.'

This thesis is persuasive. The brain drain, a kind of demographic flight of capital, has had devastating effects on countries such as China, India and the former Soviet Union. It was of considerable importance in the collapse of East Germany. A large proportion of the Iranian intelligentsia has emigrated in recent decades. The number of doctors from the Third World working in Western Europe exceeds the number of aid workers who are sent to Asia, Africa and Latin America—where there is a shortage of trained doctors everywhere—from the states of the European Community.

The better qualified the immigrants, the fewer

reservations they encounter. The Indian astrophysicist, the star Chinese architect, the Black African Nobel Prize-winner are welcome all over the world. The rich are also never mentioned in this context; no one questions their freedom of movement. For businessmen from Hong Kong the acquisition of a British passport is no problem. For immigrants from any country, Swiss citizenship, too, is only a matter of price. No one has ever objected to the colour of the Sultan of Brunei's skin. Where bank accounts look healthy, xenophobia disappears as if by magic. But strangers are all the stranger if they are poor.

In this respect the drug and arms dealers, together with the banks which launder their money, put everyone else in the shade. They recognize no distinctions of race or nationality. These are probably the only people in the world who are quite without prejudice.

XX

OF COURSE, the poor are not a homogeneous society either. In all rich countries there are complicated procedures for the control of immigration. They favour those among the poor with very particular characteristics which are valued under capitalism, such as knowledge of the world, determination, flexibility and criminal energies. These virtues are indispensable in overcoming bureaucratic obstacles. In other situations, however, sheer physical strength counts. It was only the youngest and strongest of the Albanians who could hold their own against the Italian authorities to the very end.

Mayo Smith again: 'On the other side, it is said that the men who are doing well at home are the ones least likely to emigrate because they have the least to gain. It is therefore the restless, the unsuccessful, or at least those not fitted for the strenuous competition of the older countries, who are tempted to go.'

That there is some truth in this is demonstrated by the credulous victims of the organized gangs which smuggle people from Asia, Africa and Eastern Europe. These travellers have not the least idea what awaits them. Once arrived at their goal, they seem apathetic, as if they had long ago abandoned all hope.

XXI

BLACK MARKETS flourish everywhere there are restrictions. Like connecting vessels, they equalize pressure between supply and demand without regard for laws, regulations and ethical norms. Since in the real world there are no completely closed systems, illegal transactions can be impeded by controls but never quite prevented. Market forces seek and find the smallest gap, the tiniest crack, and eventually slip through every barrier.

So an illegal trade in human beings has developed in all wealthy countries. However, whereas in classic black markets higher prices are always obtained than in legal trade, the black market in labour obeys the reverse logic. Lack does not rule here, but superfluity. Superfluous people are cheap. Clandestine immigration reduces the price of labour.

Each illegally employed immigrant presupposes an illegally operating entrepreneur. The shadow economy usually works hand in glove with the criminal gangs and networks that smuggle human beings. In the textile industry, parts of the service sector and, above all, the building trade, practices dominate which are reminiscent of the slave markets of the past.

In some parts of the United States and in the Mediterranean countries of Europe, the shadow economy has so much political power that it is in a position to exert considerable pressure on the administration. In Germany also, the authorities often turn a blind eye to illegal employment. Regulations supposed to stem immigration are surreptitiously sabotaged, and curious forms of compromise arise.

Inevitably the size of these slave markets is unknown. No one has any interest in discovering it. The only certain thing is that the numbers involved are very large. In the United States, estimates suggest there are several million illegal immigrants, mostly from Mexico; in Italy, the figure must be well over a million. Wherever one looks closely it becomes evident that the officially proclaimed 'policy towards foreigners' rests on a series of deliberate self-deceptions.

XXII

DOES THE Great Migration represent a solution, and if so, to which problem? Would Albania, for example, be helped if the active half of its population was admitted to other countries? 'It is evident that no general answer can be given to this question.' That is the conclusion to which Richmond Mayo Smith came a hundred years ago. Today, there is little else to add.

XXIII

THE DEITY of Asylon granted the gift of immunity to any innocent man who was persecuted, especially strangers in the land, but also to whomever was burdened with the guilt of murder—so anulling the continuity of blood revenge. These are the origins of the secondary political and social development of the idea of asylum in the utilitarian sense of a system of law no longer predominantly bound by religion. This no longer granted asylum to all, but only to certain persons . . . as a privilege dictated by state and economic interests and requiring diplomatic recognition by decree. It therefore guaranteed, in the interest of international trade, the protection of the stranger, who was otherwise practically without rights.

Der kleine Pauly. Munich 1975. Vol. I, page 671.

Asylum is an ancient convention of sacred origin. It owes its name to the Greeks, though the convention can also be demonstrated in other tribal societies, for example among the Jews. It also survived during the Middle Ages: criminals and debtors who had taken refuge in a church could be delivered up to secular justice only with the consent of the bishop. In more recent times, this custom has been increasingly restricted, first in the Protestant countries, and with the modern legal code it has disappeared altogether.

In international law, embassies were the first places of asylum, a tradition maintained until today notably in Latin America. From the expanded concept of sovereignty, nation states derived the right to take in foreigners, who were being politically persecuted in their homeland, and to refuse to surrender them. Yet asylum is not the individual right of the refugee but of the receiving state which admits him. Representative cases of this practice include the rebellious Poles, as well as revolutionaries such as Garibaldi, Kossuth, Louis Blanc, Bakunin and Mazzini, who were regarded as criminals in their countries of origin but often celebrated as heroes in the countries that took them in.

The refugees, whom in Germany we call asylum-seekers or *Asylanten*—asylants, usually have little in common with such historical figures. Contemporary linguistic usage is influenced by a meaning the word assumed in the Victorian period:

> The most frequently occurring asylums, the need for which makes itself felt chiefly in the great cities, are the following: i) for drunkards (inebriates' homes); ii) for prostitutes (often called Magdalene Foundations); iii) for released prisoners, who are lacking employment; iv) for poor women in childbed; v) asylums for the homeless.

These are the antiquated expressions of a reference work from the turn of the century.

Such places of custody have nothing to do with the original meaning of asylum. They are intended not for foreigners, but for stigmatized locals. The only thing these people have in common is poverty.

XXIV

THE IDEA of asylum has always been ambiguous. Expediency and religiously determined ethics have become fused so that it is difficult to separate them again. In the beginning were robbery, murder and killing. Within one's clan there was no other sanction but the endless chain of revenge, and whoever did not belong had no rights at all. Asylum—etymologically, the place where one was not robbed—was a makeshift, created in order to meet a need and to make communication and exchange beyond tribal boundaries possible.

The immunity of asylum necessarily held good for both guilty and innocent, criminals and victims alike, and the moral ambiguity is evident even to the present day. One only needs to think of figures such as Pol Pot in Peking, Idi Amin in Libya, Marcos in Hawaii or Stroessner in Brazil, to say nothing of the numerous Nazis, who, with the help of the Vatican, found refuge in Latin America. Originally this practice may have represented an attempt to provide overthrown rulers with the option of retreat, lessening the risk of civil war. As the Cambodian example shows, however, the granting of asylum can also serve the aim of keeping conflicts alive. At any rate, the 'noble' asylum-seeker is a nineteenth-century idea. In historical perspective he is the exception.

XXV

CONFUSING THE right to asylum with other questions of immigration and emigration has fatal consequences. The social and political expansion of the concept of asylum has made the muddle even greater. It is not clear why immigrants should be equated with overthrown dictators and criminals on the run, nor with alcoholics and tramps. The result is that 'asylum-seeker' has become a discriminatory, negatively loaded term, a political football.

This deliberately engineered confusion, however, turns against those who practise it, because it contradicts the fundamental idea of asylum to separate the good from the bad according to the motto: I decide who is a 'genuine' asylum-seeker and who is not. This is simply not possible, even with the best will in the world—which can hardly be assumed. The distinction between economic refugees and victims of political persecution has become an anachronism in many countries. A state of law which tries to make the distinction will inevitably be embarrassed, since it is increasingly difficult to deny that the impoverishment of whole continents has political causes, and that internal and external factors can no longer be clearly distinguished.

After all, the diffuse world war between winners and losers is carried out not only with bombs and automatic rifles. Corruption, indebtedness, flight of capital, hyper-inflation, exploitation, ecological catastrophes, religious fanaticism and sheer incompetence can reach a level which provides just as solid reasons for flight as the direct threat of prison, torture or shooting. All administrative procedures which aim to distinguish irreproachable from improper asylum-seekers must fail for that reason alone.

GERMANY IS a country that owes its present population to huge movements of migration. Since earliest times there has been a constant exchange of population groups for the most diverse reasons. As a consequence of their geographical position alone, the Germans, like the Austrians, are a very mixed people. That blood- and race-ideologies became politically dominant here, of all places, can be understood as a form of compensation. The Aryan was never anything more than a risible construct. (To that extent German racism is different from Japanese racism which appeals to the relatively high degree of ethnic homogeneity of the island population.) A cursory glance at a historical atlas is enough to show that the idea of a compact German population is unfounded. Its function can only be to prop up, by means of a fiction, an especially fragile national identity.

The recent history of the country bears witness to exactly that. The Second World War mobilized the Germans in more than one sense. Not only did the majority of the male population swarm out as far as the North Cape and the Caucasus (and, as prisoners of war, as far as Siberia and New England), and not only did Fascism force substantial elements of the German élite and almost the whole Jewish population into emigration or to their deaths. During the war, nearly ten million forced labourers, a third of them women, were abducted to Germany from all over Europe, so that thirty per cent of all jobs, and in the armaments industry more than half, were filled by foreigners. After the war, they were followed by millions of displaced persons; only a very few of them, however, remained in Germany.

Further large-scale migrations began at the end of the war. The number of refugees who, between 1945 and 1950, came into the four occupation zones is estimated at twelve million; in addition there were more than three million 'resettlements' of people from Eastern Europe and the Soviet Union who were considered to be of German origin. Between 1944 and 1989, 4.4 million went to the West from the former East Germany. Then, in the mid-fifties, the systematic recruitment of labour migrants began, which is the principal reason for more than five million foreigners having their legal place of residence in Germany. (The proportion of foreigners is still well below the level of ten per cent which, if one includes the Poles from the Prussian eastern provinces, was recorded before the First World War.)

Until the eighties, the right to asylum was an infinitesimally minor factor in population movements. But from 1955 to 1986, between 400,00 and 600,000 Germans emigrated every year, a fact which, remarkably, is ignored in political debate.

It is puzzling that a population that has lived through such times can suffer from the delusion that the current migrations are an unprecedented phenomenon. It is as if Germans had fallen victim to the amnesia observed in the railway passenger scenario. To a large extent they are new arrivals, who themselves have only just secured a seat, but insist on enjoying the rights of those who have been there for ever. As is well known, the consequences go beyond a reluctance to move closer together in the first-class compartment. Since 1991 they have reached the dimensions of an organized manhunt.

XXVII

IS XENOPHOBIA a specifically German problem? If that were so, it would be too good to be true—the solution would be obvious: isolate the Federal Republic, and the rest of the world could heave a sigh of relief. It would be easy to point to some neighbouring countries where immigration is dealt with more rigorously and where entry quotas are lower than in Germany. But such comparisons are unproductive. Xenophobia is a universal phenomenon. The irrationality of the controversy is not specifically German, since nowhere does the subject seem easily accessible to reason. What, then, is so special about the Germans? Why has such an extreme polarization emerged here?

The historical guilt felt by the Germans, no matter how well founded, is not a sufficient explanation. The causes go further back. They lie in the precarious self-consciousness of the nation. It is a fact that Germans like neither each other nor themselves; the emotions which came to the surface with German unification leave no doubt about that. But someone who dislikes himself is going to find it difficult to love those who are not even his neighbours.

This is evident not only in the hostility towards foreigners, which, from the denial of obvious facts ('Germany is not a country of immigration') to the mobilization of gangs of thugs, has formed a continuum, but also from the opposition to it.

Nowhere is a universalist rhetoric more highly valued than in Germany. Immigrants are defended in a moralizing tone of utter self-righteousness: slogans such as 'Foreigners, don't leave us alone with the Germans!' or

130

'Never again Germany!' testify to a sanctimonious reversal of signs. The racist cliché appears in the negative. Immigrants are idealized in a manner reminiscent of philo-Semitism. Taken far enough, the inversion of prejudice can become discrimination against the majority. Self-hatred is projected on to others—notably in the insidious assertion 'I am a foreigner', which numerous German celebrities have adopted.

A curious alliance between the remnants of the Left and the clergy has emerged. (Similar alliances can also be observed in Scandinavia, which suggests that the stance has something to do with the political culture of Protestantism). Preaching the Sermon on the Mount is surely a duty of the church. Ineffectiveness cannot be an objection in the context of religion. Professing it only becomes hypocrisy when it passes itself off as a political solution. Whoever calls upon his fellow citizens to offer shelter to the weary and wretched of the earth—often with reference to collective crimes stretching from the conquest of America to the Holocaust—without consideration of the consequences, without regard for political and economic mediations or whether such a project is realizable, loses all credibility. He becomes incapable of action. Deep-seated social conflicts cannot be abolished by sermons.

Evidently a disorientated Left, in defiance of its classic texts and despite the disastrous consequences of years of self-deception, still clings to the superstition that a recalcitrant being will, after all, submit to correct consciousness if only it is drummed into people often enough. That a self-declared minority of the righteous wants a different nation for itself may correspond to its pedagogic ambition. But a change of heart will hardly be achieved through blackmail. To paraphrase Brecht, 'Would it not be easier/In that case for the preachers/To dissolve the people/And elect another?'

XXVIII

A FONDNESS for principles is a traditional weakness of German intellectuals. It leads to constant and excessive ethical demands on oneself and to a recurring loss of credibility. There is, however, yet another disagreeable aspect. It is difficult enough for Germans to come to terms with themselves and their neighbours. Yet the same self-righteous moralists who would welcome all the needy of the earth are simultaneously demanding that the villains of yesterday become a model of altruism for everyone else, so that the problems of the Second and Third Worlds can be mended by the contrite German soul. In this case, too, the idea is embarrassed as soon as it comes into conflict with any concrete interest; but when politics is conducted in this way, embarrassment is the least significant problem to arise.

XXIX

IT IS always impossible to predict how many immigrants a country can accommodate for it is not simply a question of absolute numbers: too many variables are involved. Social and psychological learning and familiarization processes cannot be arbitrarily speeded up. With unpractised populations abrupt quota increases can produce semi-allergic reactions.

Economic analysis, however, offers the best objective guidelines. The unavoidable conflicts that arise from large-scale migration only intensified when unemployment became chronic in the host countries. In times of full employment, which will probably never return, millions of labour migrants were recruited. Almost ten million immigrants came to the United States from Mexico; three million to France from the Maghreb; five million to Germany, among them almost two million Turks. The migration was not merely tolerated, it was welcomed. The mood only changed as unemployment increased, despite a simultaneous growth in prosperity. Since then the immigrant's opportunities on the labour market have sunk dramatically. Many are facing a career on welfare. In the face of virtually insurmountable bureaucratic barriers, others have to live illegally. The only prospects open to them are the shadow economy and criminality: prejudice becomes a self-fulfilling prophecy.

XXX

A FURTHER structural obstacle to immigration, the importance of which is underestimated, is the welfare state. In contrast with America, where no newcomer can count on a social net to catch him, the inhabitants of many European states can at least claim minimal safeguards such as unemployment benefit, healthcare and social security. In principle these rights cannot be refused to foreigners.

However, where both individual and collective assets are regarded as sacred, the readiness to extend solidarity to foreigners is limited. The trade unions and social–

democratic parties also have to compromise, as the welfare state comes under ever greater pressure. The existing systems of safeguards are conceived as associations of paying members; their time scale is short, their long-term financing uncertain.

There is little point in trying to demonstrate that the newcomers are not only users but also contributors to the welfare state, or that immigration can have a beneficial effect on the age structure of the population. The condition for that would be a labour market able to absorb immigrants. In any case, many demographers believe that the hope of such a harmonization is an illusion. Immigration would have to reach enormous proportions in order to restore the traditional age pyramid. Depending on the model used, it has been estimated that the United States would require four to ten million and Germany at least one million young immigrants *every year*, for this goal to be achieved. There is nothing to suggest that the latter could cope with such an influx, either politically or economically.

XXXI

FROM A subjective viewpoint, things look even worse. A readiness and capacity for integration can no longer be assumed in any country or group. The multicultural society remains a confusing slogan as long as the difficulties which it throws up, and fails to clarify, remain taboo. The wearisome dispute will never be resolved if no one knows, or wants to know, what culture means—'Everything that humans do and do not do' seems the most precise definition. For this reason alone, the debate is condemned to reproduce the contradiction between deliberate underestimation and denunciation, idyll and panic.

The experiences provided by large-scale migrations in the past are ignored in such discussions. The opponents of immigration deny the examples of success which could be found everywhere, from the Swedes in Finland to the Huguenots in Prussia and elsewhere, from the Poles in the Ruhr to the Hungarian refugees of 1956. The advocates will not hear of the risks. They refuse to take account of the civil wars in the Lebanon, in the former Yugoslavia and in the Caucasus, or the conflicts in the American cities. The idea of a multinational state has seldom proved durable. It is perhaps asking too much that anyone remember the disintegration of the Ottoman Empire or the Habsburg Monarchy. But as far as the former Soviet Union is concerned, no knowledge of history is required; a television is enough. The Soviet Union made great efforts to instil a sense of identity and of common goals in a 'multicultural society'. The result was an implosion with incalculable consequences.

Dangers can also be observed in the classic countries of immigration. New arrivals traditionally showed themselves extremely willing to adapt, even if it is doubtful that the famous 'melting pot' ever existed. Most were well able to distinguish between integration and assimilation. They accepted the written and unwritten norms of the society which took them in, but they tended to hold on to their cultural tradition—and often also to their language and religious customs.

Today it is impossible to count on such an attitude among the old minorities or the new immigrants. More and more frequently common bonds are being renounced. Poverty and discrimination have led minorities, especially in the United States, but also in Great Britain and France, to adopt aggressive political ideologies. The excluded have turned the tables and are cutting themselves off. Ever more groups in the population are insisting on their 'identity'. It is by no means clear what this is supposed to mean. Militant spokesmen raise separatist demands. At times, the slogans fall back on the legacy of tribalism. There is talk of a black 'nation' and an Islamic 'nation'. In England, Pakistani fundamentalists have set up a 'Muslim Parliament' on the grounds that the Islamic population of the country constitutes a political system of its own. Conspiracy theories attract a mass following; many blacks in the United States believe that the drug trade is a calculated strategy of the whites with the aim of exterminating the black minority.

There are confrontations not only with the majority, but also between the minorities. African-Americans fight against Jews, Latinos against Koreans, Haitians against local blacks and so on. Social conflicts become nationalized. In some city districts there are virtual tribal wars. In extreme cases apartheid is claimed as a human right and the conversion of the ghetto into a separate state is elevated into an ultimate goal. Nevertheless, the spokesmen for these movements are demagogues without democratic legitimacy, and it does not look as though the masses which they supposedly represent stand behind them.

XXXII

EVEN IF the immigrants' readiness to integrate is decreasing, it is not they who provoke conflict, but those who think of themselves as natives. If only it were just the *déclassé*, the skinheads and neo-Nazis! But the gangs form only the violent, self-appointed vanguard of xenophobia. The goal of integration has not yet been accepted by large parts of the European population. The majority is not ready for it, at present perhaps not even capable of it.

One recent argument against immigration derives from the arsenal of anti-colonialism. Algeria for the Algerians, Cuba for the Cubans, Tibet for the Tibetans, Africa for the Africans—such slogans which helped many liberation movements to victory are now also being taken up by Europeans, which is not without a certain insidious logic.

It is possible to see the project of a 'preventive migration policy', which is intended to remove the causes of emigration, as a philanthropic variant of this idea. For that to succeed, the gap between rich and poor countries would need to be eliminated or at least reduced considerably. The task is beyond the economic capacity of the industrial nations, even leaving aside the matter of the ecological limits to growth. Besides, the political will for global redistribution cannot be discerned anywhere. Half a century of so-called development policies make all hope of such an about-face appear utopian. In 1925, Imre Frenczi, a League of Nations official, asked how 'there can ever be a uniform distribution of people on the earth whose traditions, standard of living and race differ so much from one another, without endangering the peace and progress of mankind'. No one has found out yet.

XXXIII

THAT ANYONE can say out loud what he thinks of the government or the state or the Lord above without being tortured and threatened with death; that disagreements are settled before a court and not by a blood feud; that women can move freely and are not forced to sell themselves or be circumcised; that one can cross the street without being caught in the machine-gun fire of rampaging soldiery: all this is not merely good, it is essential. Throughout the world there are people, presumably the majority, who desire such conditions, and are ready to defend them where they exist. These are the minimum prerequisites of civilization.

In the history of humanity this minimum has been achieved only exceptionally and temporarily. Whoever wants to defend it from external challenges faces a dilemma: the more fiercely civilization defends itself against an external threat and puts up barriers around itself, the less, in the end, it has left to defend. But, as far as the barbarians are concerned, we need not expect them at the gates. They are always already with us.

Certain Peculiarities Concerning the Manhunt

ANYONE WHO intervenes in the political discourses of German public life does so at his own risk. It is not so much the moral accusations usual in this sphere, which are a deterrent (they draw on an established tradition and are a familiar feature of journalism); more serious are the intellectual risks taken by someone who participates in a media debate. He will almost inevitably be made to look foolish as soon as he makes a contribution. The reason is not hard to find: whoever submits to the premises of a chat show is already lost, and has only himself to blame. It is no secret where the rules, to which the participants more or less cheerfully subordinate themselves, come from.

Years ago, word got round the party headquarters that the occupation of ideas is strategically just as important as control of the apparatus of power. One has to admire the skill with which the political class, for which nothing is less congenial than an idea, has made this theory its own. One consequence is that political debate is becoming more and more of a media phantom; it evaporates on television, and especially television is at its dreariest: the daily news report on political developments in Bonn. The discourse of the opposition is also restricted by such conditions: it contents itself by turning its opponent's slogans upside down.

Nowhere does this crude pattern emerge more clearly than in the 'policy towards foreigners' and the 'asylum debate'. The very formulations are obviously products of the Bonn muck heap. Politicians have, however, managed to displace the argument on to two areas which can be arbitrarily interchanged as required. On the one hand, an abstract moralizing discussion of principles is instigated; on the other, it is possible, at any time, to fall back on issues of legal procedure as soon as the question of putting anything into practice is raised. With this double strategy, quite obvious questions, which the promoters are evidently not interested in asking, fall by the wayside.

I would like to raise one such question here, which though it is not central to the problem of the Great Migration, is, nevertheless, a matter of life and death for those who already live in Germany—whatever their passport or stamp or legitimacy. It is the question of whether the country is actually habitable. I call a place uninhabitable where a gang of thugs is free to attack people in the middle of the street or set fire to their homes.

One can disregard the question of who is and who is not supposed to be German, at least as long as it is not decided by having one group wear normal clothes, while the rest are forced by law to stick triangles, crosses or stars on themselves. Since no one has so far proposed such laws, the distinction between natives and foreigners is irrelevant in this context. It is also superfluous, in this context, to distort sentimentally the status of the foreigner, for example with the popular assertion which is being proclaimed by every would-be celebrity: 'I am a foreigner.'

Even the briefest glance reveals that swindlers and bores, louts and idiots are encountered among the native population with the same statistical frequency as among Turks, Tamils and Poles. Being forced to live together with them without resorting to violence is an unreasonable demand, which in a civilized society everyone without exception has to put up with. Even those who do not want to accept it, must, if necessary, be compelled to do so. For what is intolerable is the presence of people who undertake individual or organized manhunts.

The simple distinction has nothing to do with the so-called foreigners' problem. Neither does it have anything to do with new regulations for asylum procedures, still less with the misery of the Third World nor with the ubiquitous racism. At stake is the monopoly of force which the state claims for itself.

One can accuse the various governments of this republic of all kinds of things, but no one can say that they ever hesitated to make use of this monopoly if it seemed threatened. On the contrary, the executive has never shown itself lacking in enthusiasm in this respect. Federal Border Guards, secret services, security task forces, police mobile rapid response units, state and federal detective departments have always been on hand with hard- and software from computer dragnets to helicopter squadrons, from identikit pictures to armoured personnel carriers. Nor has the legislature been any less diligent. It has been game to the point of irresponsibility, constantly breaking new legal ground from the construct of the 'criminal association' to the law allowing bans on visits and letters to prisoners awaiting trial. As a result, the state has access to a terrifying arsenal of means of self-protection.

In recent months not even the least significant use has been made of these resources. Indeed, the apparatus of repression, from the police to the courts, has responded to the appearance on a massive scale of gangs of thugs in both parts of Germany with an unprecedented degree of restraint. Arrests have been the exception; where they have been carried out, the culprits have almost always been set free the following day. The Federal State Prosecutor's Office and the Federal CID, once omnipresent in the media, devoted to repelling any threats to the German people, have kept quiet, as if they had been temporarily retired. The Federal Border Guards, which only a few years ago occupied every second crossroads, seem to have disappeared from the face of the earth.

As for the politicians, many of them have taken the stage in an unfamiliar role: as social workers. Their therapeutic efforts were not directed at the hunted—they were fobbed off with high-flown phrases—but at the very people who were engaged in the manhunt. Regrettable deficiencies in the education system, especially in the former GDR, have been mentioned; there have been pleas for an understanding of the harsh reality of unemployment; besides their immaturity, the killers' cultural disorientation was taken into account. All in all, we were dealing with 'poor souls' who had to be treated with the utmost patience. It was hardly possible to expect such underprivileged persons to realize that setting fire to children is, strictly speaking, not permissible. Attention must be drawn all the more urgently to the inadequate supply of leisure activities available to the arsonists.

Such heartfelt sympathy is astonishing, when one remembers the pictures from Brokdorf (a power station which became the focus of anti-nuclear protest) and Startbahn West (a runway at Frankfurt Airport, intended primarily for US military use, whose construction was delayed by years of protest). At that time, those in power did not appear to regard the rapid development of discothèques and youth clubs as providing the solution; evidently in the seventies, uncontested free access to the paradise of leisure society had not yet become an inalienable right. On the contrary, beating, kicking and shooting were carried out with considerable vigour and, if I remember rightly, the state was quite prepared to take a couple of dead in its stride.

Is the sudden change of heart due to a conversion? Since the Enlightenment, there have always been humanitarians who have assured us that criminal law is unsuitable as a solution to social problems. That can hardly be denied, given the conditions in the jails and the high rate of recidivism, even if the reformers still owe us a convincing alternative. However, that does not explain the puzzling shift of the state apparatus towards sympathetic lenience for killers. Shoplifters and bank robbers, confidence tricksters and embezzlers, terrorists and extortionists are being sent down as they always have been; no political party has as yet advocated the abolition of the penal code or, even, a thorough reform of the penal system. We therefore have to turn to other explanations to understand the discrepancy between enthusiastic prosecution on the one hand, and *laissez faire* on the other.

Is it possible that the intensity of the effort depends on the interests which the law exists to protect? In the precedents already mentioned, it was a matter of the private ownership of real estate, of the right to enlarge airports, build motorways and erect nuclear installations of every kind. In the attacks and arson of recent months, however, the lives of a few thousand inhabitants of the country have been at stake. Evidently the agencies of the state consider murder and manslaughter a mere breach of the law, while the removal of a fence is a serious crime.

The circumstances also invite other interpretations. It is difficult to believe, but it cannot be quite excluded that there are politicians who sympathize with the murderous gangs roaming the country. Perhaps more likely is that many sit back and watch the manhunt impassively because they imagine that such an attitude could be politically advantageous. One does not, of course, like to believe in such a degree of idiocy, and only the absence of other plausible explanations justifies considering it.

Even the most stupid person should grasp one thing: renouncing the state's monopoly of force has consequences which may harm the political class itself. One result is a need for self-defence. If the state refuses to protect them, threatened individuals or groups will have to arm themselves. International trade will effortlessly meet the required demand. As soon as a resistance has been organized, there will be gang wars (a development that can already be observed in big cities like Berlin and Hamburg). Politically there may lead to conditions such as those Germany experienced towards the end of the Weimar Republic.

Furthermore, if mass terror on the streets has no effect, it will eventually turn against the political class. No personal security is perfect, and it would be an illusion to believe that the all-German hit-squads will, in the long term, continue to reciprocate the paternal indulgence which is extended to them in many places. Such tolerance, which always favours the criminals and never the victims, is evidence of an excessive taste for continuity. Certain politicians clearly have difficulty breaking with it. That allows several conclusions, only one of which is surprising: the sense of self-preservation of these people is less pronounced than we think.